THE JUSTIFICATION OF GOD

THE JUSTIFICATION OF GOD

Lectures for War-Time on a Christian Theodicy

BY

P. T. FORSYTH, M.A., D.D.

PRINCIPAL OF HACKNEY COLLEGE, HAMPSTEAD

Wipf & Stock
PUBLISHERS
Eugene, Oregon

Wipf and Stock Publishers
199 West 8th Avenue, Suite 3
Eugene, Oregon 97401

The Justification of God
Lectures for War-Time on a Christian Theodicy
By Forsyth, P.T.
ISBN: 1-57910-219-0
Publication date 2/23/1999
Previously published by Charles Scribner's Sons, 1917

PREFACE

I HAVE been warned that the appearance of an unfamiliar word like Theodicy on the title-page (even in the sub-title) may raise a certain prejudice in some minds that one would rather attract than repel. But it is hard to believe that the word can be so strange at a time when the passion for the thing has, by the magnitude of our present calamity, become for multitudes the keynote of their religion. We are all familiar more or less with one noble work, equally of faith and of art, whose object was stated on its front to be

> To vindicate Eternal Providence,
> And justify the ways of God to man.

That is a theodicy, the attempt to adjust the ways of God to conscience. But to His own conscience above all. That is the way taken in this book. Its object is not to bring God's ways to the bar either of man's reason or man's conscience, but rather to the bar where all reason and conscience must go at last, to the standard of a holy God's own account of Himself in Jesus Christ and His Cross. A philosophical theodicy or vindication of God's justice has not yet been found. And if faith wait for it, the soul may perish first. But a religious and theological theodicy (for here the one means the other) is not only not impossible; it is our only refuge. This is the kind of theology that retains much public interest or promise to-day—the justification of God by Himself, and not by a course of history which is a dim mixture of His ways and our ways, and where the cross lights make it impossible to see life steadily and see it whole. The only vindicator of God is God. And His own theodicy is in the Cross of His Son Jesus Christ. The problem of God is the problem of history and of God in it. The doubts that unsettle men most to-day are those that rise not from science but from society, not from the irrational but the unjust. And the very nature of that question is a great step to the answer. Every great question is pointed in proportion as it is moralised—as we are made to discuss business rather than being, the doings rather than the laws of the world, soul rather than substance, and the conscience rather than the processes either of God or man. It will then be found that the justification of God to man is not possible except to the conscience of man as justified by God. We have God's justice as a gift and not as a conclusion. God vindicates His justice by saving man from the doubt of it, and not by demonstrating to him the truth of it.

I have to express my thanks to my colleague, Rev. H. H. Scullard, D.D., for his kind service in revising proof.

P. T. FORSYTH.

August 1916.

CONTENTS

CHAPTER VII

CHAPTER VIII

CHAPTER IX

CHAPTER X

CHAPTER XI

CHAPTER XII

THEODICY

OVERTURE AND OUTLINE

In the crowd of modern problems the individual Christian may be content to leave everything simply and happily to the love of God, his Saviour, who has done for his past and present what may well be trusted with his future. But we cannot stop there. In the first place, the question at all great crises is not one of a soul's future but of the world's. The problem of his kind has laid hold of the Christian soul. 'Lord, and what shall this race do ?' is a very Christian concern. And, in the next place, if the Christian man may rest in a very plain faith, the Christian Church cannot. The consciousness of the Church has the spiritual imagination. Its conscience is in the great style. Eternity is set in its heart, to say nothing of the note of Humanity. It thinks and feels both humanly and on the scale of Eternity. And one of the sources of difficulty and confusion to-day is that problems of the Church, collective problems, are constantly being treated amateurly, that is on the mere individual scale, with a mere individual instinct, or a mere individual piety, and often without a due individual equipment. They are treated without the trained historic sense, or the universal and ethical, or the theological and eternal, without more than the domestic range of concern, whose ethic is but in the primary colours. Of course (though it is hard for any to evade these larger questions to-day) the individual need not always raise them ; and to some it may be a dangerous hobby. But the Church must raise them, or at least it must face them when raised. It must have members, servants, and leaders who can do both competently. The Church, indeed, begins and ends with a Gospel which contemplates and provokes questions on that scale. And, if the individual raise such issues, it must be with the Church mind, it must be on the scale of the world as a whole, which, and nothing less, is the great Church's *vis-à-vis*.[1] The inability to do this on the part of modern individualism is a chief source of the distaste for theology, and especially for St. Paul, who always envisaged the individual soul in the universal salvation. He was therefore constantly misunderstood, as Jesus Himself was; but neither for that reason changed his note, because the obscurity was in the matter rather than the style, and was therefore charged by them upon the spiritual density of their audience and not upon their own literary ineptness. Jesus spoke, and kept speaking, as to wise men; and Paul constantly strove to speak wisdom among adult and not trivial minds, and on the scale not of the world only but of God (1 Cor. ii. 6). He prayed without ceasing that his recent converts might be filled with the knowledge of God's will in all wisdom and understanding (Col. i. 9), and that they might know the wealth of the magnificent legacy they had as men and members of Christ, who is Head of all things, and the fullness of both worlds (Eph. i. fin.). The problems of the private life are often so intractable because they are not conceived in any but private relations; which is to judge the house from a sample brick. The manna so hoarded goes wrong. The soul's lot lies in the eternal and universal counsel of God. And the first question still is man's chief end, and the collective destiny of every

[1] It was this true Churchliness of the sects that took effect in their invention of modern missions at the beginning of the nineteenth century. Foreign missions was the Church in them saving itself from the sects, the world note saving them from the note worldly and bourgeois.

soul there. The eternal does not begin on the other side of time; rather all time and space is the content of eternity. Faith is really faith in that eternal destiny as present, and then in our part and place therein by God's grace. Immortality means living on in Eternity; it is Eternity living on in us. It is God thinking Himself, living Himself in us. But we are apt to treat God as if He were only a patron saint magnified, whom we expect to attend to our affairs if He is to retain our custom and receive our worship.

There is even what we might call a racial egoism, a self-engrossment of mankind with itself, a naïve and tacit assumption that God were no God if He cared for anything more than He did for His creatures. We tend to think of God as if man were His chief end, as if He had no right to a supreme concern for His own holy name, as if His prodigals were more to Him than His only begotten Son in whom He made the worlds and has all His delight. We think and worship as if the only question was whether God loves us, instead of whether His love has absolute power to give itself eternal and righteous effect. Modern science is especially prone to remind us of this egoism latent in Christian faith, and is eager to prune it. Accordingly we are told of the infinities of space and time, amid which our earth and its history swim but as a mote in the air; and we are urged, with such knowledge, to moderate our ideas of a future, and our expectations of divine attention. Now, though science is wrong in asking us to suppress our soul or conscience before world on world of spacial or temporal existence (because the spiritual is not spacial), yet the advice is not without value. There are considerations which should quell a crude, racial egoism, and should lift mankind out of the self-absorption which blights and shrivels the individual. But they are not considerations of the Creation but of its Creator, not of a Universe but of a Sovereign God, who is so much to us because He is more to Himself, and whose love is infinite because it is holy, and it must be hallowed, even if He spare not His Son. His Son spared not Himself in the hallowing of that name. It was the first function of His Cross. And so He was Saviour—because He loved God more than man, and glorified His name over all weal of ours. We have no final weal but our share in that worship and glory of the Father by the Son.

A world catastrophe and judgment of the first rank like the present war is still in the hand and service of God, in so far as it forces the soul through its individual faith into concern about a world providence and a world salvation. How do we stand to-day to the old dilemma, 'If He has power to stop these things and does not, He is not good; if He is good, and does not, He has not power'? It is well that a soul's solitary religion should be driven to be a solidary and racial, that the cell should realise the hive, that atomic belief should widen to a common faith. It is well that even a group-faith should rise to the faith of a Church, and that a Church's message should be enlarged to face a world crisis, and roused to the dimensions of a world Gospel and a Majesty divine.

Village politics and village piety have been set aside for the moment by the question of Europe and of civilisation. And it was time. For thought was raising much larger questions than a kindly and pedestrian piety could cope with—questions not only beyond the dear old piety of Hodge, but also beyond the new piety of culture, with its mild anti-theology, and its modest discipleship where we need a bold and humble apostolate. The nemesis of an anti-theological religion is that it has no resources in a crisis except pale quietism or ruddy patriotism. It follows the saint or the drum. It retires among mystics, or it goes out with a flushed nationalism. But its scale of business cannot handle large orders. It has not resources for a foreign trade. It gravitates to the retail business. It has more instinct for missions, for instance, than power to maintain them or manage them. It deals with the minor matters which (so to say) draw only on the intelligence and tact of the travellers; it has not a policy which reflects the genius of the partners and directors in a vast concern. To drop metaphor, the attractive piety of incipient culture, with its atmosphere of young bustle, good form, gentle faith, genial love, kindly conference, and popular publications, is without the great note of New Testament realism and imagination; and it is therefore at an utter loss when all the world is shocked and forced upon the question of a theodicy. What can it do in the swellings of Jordan? It applies the commonplaces of a pacific Christianity offhand to world movements, with a grasp neither of the Gospel nor of the world. 'Too white, for the flower of life is red.'

From these we turn in vain to the philosophers of a larger horizon, whose ideal theories and optimist hopes from an expanding evolution or a spiritual refinement have received such a shattering blow. Optimism is then found not to be the same thing as courage. On the other hand, the pessimists, who were looked on as cranks, especially by the established philosophers, find their account richly in the situation—the people whose whole view of life rests on the denial of any possible theodicy or moral solution, and ends in cosmic dissolution.

The effect of the present unparalleled disaster to the world is that of every judgment of God. It will sift and part. Many who are but lightly persuaded Christians will drop out, as if a man had leaned on a wall and a snake from it bit him. It will make those who doubted and challenged to deny and despair, especially if they shirked action and hung back from the field; and it will make many of those who believed but in progress, or trusted but on traditional grounds, and were only comforted but never captured by their belief, try to believe harder still on their old lines. While the elect, renouncing a systematic apology, will take great words, and say (with the supreme empiricist of Grace), 'Even so, Father, so it hath seemed good in Thy sight.' But what was within that word of sublime humility and victory? And what came from its heart to be the word of His very apostolate, who were the intimate trustees of His final world revelation? What is His message in those who have some right to speak from the *penetralia* of the Church and its Bible? How do they answer the very natural question of the public, whether we can still believe in God's government of the world and His destiny for it? It is a question so deeply natural that it is beyond nature (unless nature can explain itself). It can have no answer outside the grace that transcends nature. It has none for those whose religion is mercy without majesty and love without either power, sanctity, or judgment. What is God's own theodicy, His final theodicy, His Self-justification to the world? What is to be our final judgment about a final judgment by God upon all such things, and within them? How are we to be saved, amid the collapse, into a belief in salvation? It is the most extreme crisis for faith—how great we do not yet realise. And the serious people will not grudge that the answer should sound extreme, that it should not be as obvious as a journal, that it come from faith and from faith's inmost citadel, and that it should seem foreign to our untaxed thought and common hours. Only an extreme position can meet an extreme situation—so long as we can make it good.

And the attempt to make it good is worth while. It is confessed scepticism of both the Church and of the Gospel, to sweep its ministry into the ranks of war. Those who are toiling in mind and suffering in spirit to provide from the Gospel, by thought, comfort, or taxing prayer, some real and staying power in the face of all the facts of the hour are not outside the soldier host who so finely answer the public need and call. They are of the combatants and not of the drones. They are angels of the Lord of Hosts, if not His captains. They are reservists against the hour when the trial of faith may become even more acute, when native courage begins to flag, and faith must be a song in the night that opens the prison-gates. To speculate at such a time on the psychology of the Trinity might be but monastic. But to re-interrogate the Word of the historic Gospel for its word to the historic time, to leave the theosophies which rule the mystic hour for a theodicy with a historic base, a moral genius, and a mystic power—that is to be a true chaplain to the Lord's host. To justify God is the best and deepest way to fortify men. It provides the moral resource and stay which is the one thing at last. With open face to see the glory of God in things as they are, to blink nothing of the terror and yet to be sure of the Kingdom of God with all our heart—that is more for the courage of man than any nationalism or any patriotism when heart fails and grief benumbs. Since the civil wars there has been no such time in England. And we came through these only upon the puritan faith which a long peace and a thin culture have now drowned delicately as in a butt of Malmsey wine.

The solution of the great world juncture is at last a religious solution. And, being a historic juncture, it concerns the Kingdom of God and God's provision for it in history. It taxes all the resources that faith has, but it settles us in a certainty which is very much in the world but not of it. The Church will come out of the present crisis both chastened and exalted if it takes itself seriously enough, and holds itself as morally greater than soul, family, or State. For it is the only society on earth whose one and direct object is the Kingdom of God—if, indeed, it be not that Kingdom in the making. There is much speculation about the situation after the war, and especially about the need for an effective international. And most of it leaves the Church out of the question, or any spiritual authority. Why ? From the sand-blindness of those without, and the uncertainty of those within it.

One of the obvious yet great ironies of life is the spectacle offered in a war which breaks in upon an unprecedented craving of Western Christianity for spiritual unity. As religion seemed to be growing more ashamed than ever before of its divisions, civilisation, always prone to mock the disunion of the Churches it has demoralised, cuts across its path with a strife such as the world has never seen. Christianity, drowsing often but never dead, and now re-awaking to its function as the human bond, is struck in the face by a paganism which is divisive and deadly on a scale never yet known. The Churches, weary of much triviality and impotence, yet unforsaken by the instinct of greatness and authority in their Gospel, were moving to recover its native note, and lead the great irenic of the race; when, suddenly, their generous, if sometimes crude, enthusiasm is shattered for the time by the crash, not only of the guns, but of the moral collapse of a leading Christian nation. The situation is alluded to here chiefly because it rouses all kinds of questions, which peace muffles in sentiment, about the brotherhood of man, the destiny of the race, the purpose of God, or even a moral order in the world. Is there such a thing as the unity of the race reflecting the unity and power of God ? Is it feasible or even credible ? Is a practicable conviction of it at present possible ? Is there any basis of human brotherhood beyond the dream that vanishes at the first shock ? Is the chief result of western civilisation to put the world's peace further off than ever before ? Is civilisation pacific in its nature, or only better than before at the bad old game ? Is human concord but a fantasy of that idealism which passes down through culture to cruelty, as in the Italian republics, and which, when it comes to historic business, seems to issue in a storm of 'frightfulness' and in the blight of that moral cynicism which dogs intellectualism ? Is there a moral order, or is the only curb on individual egoism a national egoism which makes a race its own God, and patriotism the sole religion, severing it completely and expressly from moral dignity or control ? Does humanism end practically in the loss of humanity ?

A crowd of such questions presses in upon us from behind all the political reconstructions so freely pursued without reference to a Kingdom of God. And they seem often to become but more acute when we do carry them into the presence of God, and consider them in the light of His supreme revelation of mastery and destiny. If man is a failure, is God too ? Is love destined to dominion ? Or, perhaps, have we understood this revelation ? Is our standard sound ? I venture to discuss this in these chapters. And I would first offer an outline, or overture in advance, of what I hope to say. In many forms my belief will appear that the site of revelation and the solution of history is to be found, not in the moral order of the world, but in its moral crisis, tragedy, and great divine *commedia* ; not even in the conscience, but in its Christ and His Cross.

It seems quite certain that it is only a living faith in the right kind of unity, unity with power, that can bring to the race public peace and concord. What is that unity, and where ? Why should we think mankind a unity ? It is not natural to the struggle for life. It is not how we begin. We begin as warring atoms. Are we to subside to the same state at the end, and die in the bed where we were born ? Is the race's unity assured us either in its origin or in its destiny ? Do we know enough about either ? Or shall we find it in the organic unity of thought, in the idea ? That line has ended in the Germany we see. Or can we take stand on the elemental emotions and passions, on the sympathies ? But is hate not the twin of love ? Does the touch of nature really make the world kin when we come to business and when interests cross ? Is it not as natural to destroy as to help ? What turns the balance to the helping side ? Or, again, with a vague and hasty faith in progress, shall we look for the index of a racial unity in the spread of civilisation and the organisation of common interests ? This last is an argument that nobody is very likely to press at present.

Shall we then turn and question the history of the race ? Is man's unity Adamic, in a common progenitor ? Is it due to a single and common creation ? Or shall we look for a plan of beneficent progress looming up through man's career ? History shows no such plan, especially in the moral region where we need it most. Mere historicism does not even give us a standard by which we can tell what is progress and what is not. If enlightenment seem emerging at any stage, it is crushed thereupon by world wars, Napoleonic or Teutonic. And it is not light for its own sake that we need, but something that light reveals. The great matter is neither the eye nor the gleam, but the thing, the reality, the soul, the power, the God. Is there a growth then in the great sympathies ? In the reign of righteousness ? We might have thought so till recently. But even then only by shutting our eyes to what Europe's armaments meant, the world-wide, competitive mammonism, the cult of material efficiency, and the growth of terrorism in the social action of, for instance, the women and the workmen. In the course of history it is hard to trace any unitary and beneficent plan of operations. War, which is the triumph of plan, is moral anarchy. Nothing is so efficient as a bomb. Civilisation, as mere organisation and machinery, ends there. It is deadly bombast (if the play were allowed) worked, like a Zeppelin, by inflation. As we become civilised, we grow in power over everything but ourselves, we grow in everything but power to control our power over everything. Man, from the land, can harness the seas to serve him, but the winds and the waves do not obey him.

Shall we, then, in search of a unity of the race, turn from questioning either human origins or the historic career? From the past shall we turn to the future? Shall we turn to seek a common destiny—a goal of values if not a scheme of operations, a meaning if not a system of the world? But if we could scarcely find a conspiracy of righteousness in the historic career we do know, shall we succeed better in speculating about the trend of a future we do not? Does the study of history breed the spirit of prophecy? If a sure past do not promise a reign of love, is there more hope from a conjectural future? Is there then some combination of past and future in our hands, of life's deep ground and its final goal? If the course of history promise little by induction, is there a point of history which does more by insight; which at once exhibits a goal both of God's purpose and man's progress, and has power to make that goal realise itself, power to make it, while goal, at the same time the active ground of the historic career? If we have no self-projected goal which is more than an ideal, have we one given, descending from God, to be within us the final principle and deep dynamic of human growth? Is it there, in a redeemed destiny, that we find a faith and a unity refused by our first origin or our long career?

Such at least is the Christian faith, which is the religion of a historic point in Christ's Cross, and of a moral point in the human conscience, with their crisis of grace and guilt. The focus of the race is moral, in the conscience. 'Morality is the nature of things.' Guilt is therefore the last problem of the race, its one central moral crisis; and the Cross that destroys it is the race's historic crisis and turning-point. Were there no sin, there would be no war. Were there no world sin, there would be no world war. War makes at least one contribution to human salvation—it is sin's apocalypse. It reveals the greatness and the awfulness of evil, and corrects that light and easy conception of it which had come to mark culture and belittle redemption. This war's revelation of human wickedness may perhaps do something to relieve us of a comely and æsthetic type of religion which is founded, not on a salvation, but on the divine excellence of that glorious creature man, and on the facilities for his evolution. It may recall us to the estimate of him presented by the very existence of Christianity as a religion, which declares his one need to be redemption.

> 'I still, to suppose that true for my part
> See reasons and reasons; this, to begin,
> 'Tis the faith that launched pointblank her dart
> At the head of a lie—taught original sin
> The corruption of man's heart.'

The final revelation of God is a redemption, and not a mere manifestation. It is something done and not just shown. And it is effected in man at the depth of his moral despair, and not at the height of his æsthetic pride and cultured insight.

All deep and earnest experience shows us, and not Christianity alone, that the unity of the race lies in its moral centre, its moral crisis, and its moral destiny. It is in the moral region that all our beneficent hopes and efforts for others wreck; we can deal with their bad luck, but not with their moral failure. It is there we find that the deepest thing in life is not an ordered process but a tragic collision and despair. 'Thou hast delivered my soul from the lowest hell.' Life is not a mere movement but a battle. And it is there that the battle must be won which carries sound culture and everything else with it. All comes back to the conscience, to a will in relation to a Will. The only universal religion is the religion of the conscience and its redemption. It is a religion of moral redemption. All its affectional power and beauty centres there, in *holy* love. And the Church is divided, and the world is at strife, because this note has been lost from Christianity, or made other than central and creative. Almost all who are driven to unfaith by the horrors of history seem to have cherished a faith based entirely on the teaching of Christ; they had been cherishing, that is, not a faith but an ideal, not a power but a programme. The Gospel owes its world power to its revealing the righteousness of God in action on the Cross (Rom. i. 16, 17). There springs the dynamic for the Christian ideal. There rises the new creation that realises it. It is a matter of righteousness. If there is a unity of the race, its source is the unity of God (that is, His moral holiness); its power is righteousness, its field is the conscience, and its warrant is in God's treatment of the conscience once for all in Christ's Cross. The root of conscience is in our sense of responsibility, our sense of being trustees and subjects—*i.e.* our sense of divine power and majesty over us. We are not here for freedom, but for responsibility. We are responsible for our very freedom. It is in his conscience then that man is one, and, above all, in what is done with his conscience by the power it owns supreme. Conscience is conscience because it owns to that power an obligation, which, as a matter of actual fact, is guilt. Morality culminates in repentance. Human unity is therefore one of deliverance. It is one of dependence, true, but of a sinner's dependence, of forgiveness, reconciliation, regeneration, the sense of a descending power and a giving, saving grace. We do not achieve unity by our resource, we receive it as a gift to our spiritual poverty, and as a creation out of our last distress of dissolution. Our destiny is found in our tragedy and not in our idyll, not in our hour of triumph but in our depth of distress. If man is one *in* conscience, he is not one *by* conscience; for by itself it reveals guilt and division. The unity is a unity effected *by* God *in* conscience, in the tragedy of our conscience, and not simply its voice or law. It is His gift of release to conscience, His reconstruction of it. It is not at last a matter of our conscience but of Christ in our conscience. It is a divine reconciliation, but a reconciliation of the conscience more even than of the affections (cp. 2 Cor. v. 19 with 21); it is a recall from guilt and not from mere coldness. And it is a reconciliation which means re-creation and not mere rehabilitation, as being the birth of a power in us and not merely the gift to us of a state. It is the reconciliation given to the conscience of the race by a holy grace, which must judge conscience, but which judges it in Christ and upon Him. This reconciliation comes to a head in our worship of a moral Redeemer, and the faith of a destiny of righteousness, which, though now working in history, is not to be traced on its course but trusted at its source in Him. Paul, in the whole of Romans, holds closely together the universality of the Gospel and the seat of its power in the righteousness of God (Rom. i. 17).

That moral certainty of God's conquering holiness is the only foundation of any faith in man's unity, when the last pinch comes. It is not in himself but in his God as his Saviour. It is his unity in a Redeemer and a Redemption, a unity not natural but supernatural, not by evolutionary career but by mortal crisis, not in the first creation but the second, not in generation but regeneration. Nothing can give us footing or hope amid the degeneration of man but his regeneration by God. God's method with evil is not prevention but cure. And this is the note of the Church, moral reconciliation, holy regeneration, upon a world scale—the new Humanity. This faith is the only condition, nay, the only creator, of Church unity; and it is the only creator, through the Church's Gospel, of the unity of the race and its peace. In the crises which shake all the foundations of society, the Church of the Gospel alone is sure of the end. Augustine wrote the *City of God* after the sack of Rome. But even the Church has neither a word to say nor a power to act except by this evangelical faith and this theological ethic. If the redeeming act of God is but a theological theme, then the Church must be as ineffectual and negligible as any community of hobbyists or essayists may be. But with a theological faith in God's real act and presence we have the world goal in advance, without such a faith we have no world goal assured; and therefore we have no world ethic, for lack of a world standard. And the ethic of the State then becomes absolute, as it is made in Germany—there being neither a holy God nor a solidary race to overrule national egoism. And yet the neglect, and even contempt, of such an evangelical ground has spread from the world into the Church itself. And so the first work before the Church is to set her own house in order, to return to the Cross as the source of the Spirit, to moralise her conceptions of a *Holy* Spirit, and, by courting anew at such a Gospel her own moral regeneration, to acquire that note of moral authority which gives practical power and historic weight to all her mystic insight and her sympathetic help. It is not help that either the Church or the world needs most. It is power. It is life. It is moral regeneration. If the greatest boon in the world is Christ's Holy Father, the greatest curse in the world is man's unfilial guilt. Whatever, therefore, undoes the guilt is the solution of the world. Everything will follow upon that peace and power. The righteousness which reconciles and secures everything is the holiness which destroys guilt in its very exposure. It is God's holy and atoning love making a new world in Christ's Cross.

This means, for the Church, not only a fresh submission of her conduct to the testing light of the Gospel, but a fresh grasp and construction of that Gospel; so as to bring, indeed, the old searching ray to bear on her deeds, but, still more, so as to create and kindle a new ideal, standard, and power of moral life in the spiritual society itself.

CHAPTER I

THE EXPECTATIONS OF POPULAR RELIGION AND THEIR FATE. RELIGION AS CENTRED ON GOD AND CENTRED ON MAN

A FIRST-RATE calamity to humanity like a European war is to the Christian insight the suicide of natural civilisation, which always tends to die dissolved in its own keen dialectic, or stupefied by its own crude surfeit. It is God in judgment of godlessness. But it must create in many minds, whose faith, perhaps, has owed more to Christian culture than to its moral Gospel, something beyond a doubt—a denial, of a God and Providence in the world. Of Providence and God, I say. When the one goes, the other goes; for there is no place for a God who reigns but does not govern. If the belief in a Providence goes, there is little occasion for belief in a God. Not as though belief in a God rested on a traceable Providence. It does not. But such belief is the only ground for trusting a Providence whose ways are beyond us and His strategy past finding out. We do not find God from His providential conduct of history. We cannot discern His plan of campaign. We cannot follow out His thought, however we trust His will. The tactics of Providence cannot be traced. His judgments pass knowledge. But, 'where God's judgments are not to be discovered, His counsel is not to be neglected' (Augustine). His purpose we have, and His heart. We have *Him*. And we find Him elsewhere than in a sustained policy of affairs—at a revelationary point of history. But at the same time, if we could find no trace of His conduct of man's career, or no possibility of it, we might well ask whether His existence was called for at all. *Cui bono?* If the victory went to the mere tutelar deity of a race, and not to the God of the Kingdom, there would be plenty of people to say at present that the world is no better for such a God.

I say it is inevitable that world calamities should encourage the denials of those who denied before. Their shock also makes sceptics of many whose belief had arisen and gone on only under conditions of fine weather, happy piety, humming progress, and of a religion drawing but on the sympathies and not the ethic of the soul, on heart without conscience. Such a result is inevitable for many, with the presuppositions that underlie much popular faith, and that have even come to dominate modern faith at levels higher than the popular. For what is the tacit understanding in current religion which leaves it at the mercy of social or other convulsions? I have hinted it in the preceding lecture. In theological language it is anthropocentric religion, which has displaced theocentric. That is to say, it is man's preoccupation with humanity and its spiritual civilisation or culture. It is the religious egoism of Humanity, *i.e.* man's absorption with himself, instead of with God, His purpose, His service, and His glory. It is a greater anxiety to have God on our side than to be upon His. We are willing to owe many things to God, only not ourselves and our destiny absolutely.

Everything has come to turn on man's welfare instead of God's worship, on man with God to help him and not on God with man to wait upon Him. The fundamental heresy of the day, now deep in Christian belief itself, is humanist. It is the humanism and humanitarianism which events are now reducing to an absurdity as a religion. This tendency may have been prepared by the Catholic principle that God became Man that man might become God, or by Pelagian synergism ; but it represents the extreme reaction, under Rousseau, from that Jesuitism and that Calvinism which, in the seventeenth century, saved religion in both camps by beginning and ending with God and His glory instead of man and his weal. Elated by our modern mastery of nature and cult of genius, and ridden by the superstition of progress (now unseated), we came to start with that excellent creature, man, his wonderful resources, his broadening freedom, his widening heart, his conquest of creation, and his expanding career. And, as with man we begin, with man we really end. God is there but to promote and crown this development of man, if there be a God at all. To this has come a Gospel of mere Fatherhood, of divine value without divine right, of God as an asset instead of a King, a God of great kindness without absolute Majesty, of swift pity without holy mercy, of sacrificing love without atoning righteousness or reigning power. 'Ye have made me to serve.' The Father is the banker of a spendthrift race. He is there to draw upon, to save man's career at the points where it is most threatened. He is a God of nothing but loving sacrifice for His son man, who, with such a Father, grows up the spoilt child that parental service without parental demand is sure to make. To that has come the Fatherhood, though for Christ its first claim, and the first petition in His prayer, was that it should be hallowed and not exploited. It was the one issue between Christ and Israel. He would sanctify God, they would use Him. They had most things in common with Christ but that object, as indeed we have. But the thing they had not wrecked all they had. They had a zeal for God, and a God benign. And to our zeal He has become a God of loving-kindness more than of loving power, of everlasting pity and no moral majesty, no holiness. He is of infinite value to us without absolute right. He is Father in a sense that leaves no room for love's severity, its searching judgment, or its absolute sovereignty with the right to make demand on man and no reason given, and no light shown on the spot. He is Father only so long as He meets the instincts and aspirations of man's heart. We are familiar with the heathen habit of beating the god who is too stingy to the worshippers' prayers. It survives in unexpected quarters at the severest strains. 'If God permit my heartbreak, He shall have no more of my faith. If He put out the light of my home, He is too heartless for my heart. If He permit the wreck, by its own unsupported weight, of anything which my heart calls so good as humanitarian civilisation, He is no God for worship of mine. How can I trust such a God ? ' There is a tale of which only the form is childish : 'I will pray to Him all this week for an engine, and if He don't give it me I shall worship idols.'

We may here impale in passing two complementary fallacies about love. First, that it is enjoyment, and not service and sacrifice. This was Bossuet's vulgar and popular error in his conflict with Fénelon. And, second, that love, when it becomes holy love, has no duties or sacrifices to itself. The correction of these two errors is the great function of Christian history, the moralisation of love. Truly, God alone knows the love of God, and how entirely we owe everything to it. But it is something else than human affection raised to infinity.

It is indeed hard to discuss such a frame of mind as I have described when it meets us in people who cannot see for tears, cannot think for heartbreak, and cannot believe for shock—their best and dearest hopes, private or public, being in ruins at their feet. There seems no God in a black world. 'If Thou hadst been here, my son, my husband had not died.'

The insistence on a heroic and theocentric faith may seem but heartless to those who are helpless in the last distress.

Let this then be said about an anthropocentric Christianity. It has its precious place and great rights. It is the first stage of sainthood. Christ, indeed, means 'God for us,' and our need, our despair, is His opportunity; but in such a way that He converts our blessings into His praise, and His Spirit does not return to Him void. That is to say, whereas we begin with 'God for us' by His grace, we end with 'We for God' by our faith. He so answers our prayer that we come to ask Him nothing, and we are lifted in self-oblivion to adore. His supreme value to us is to lift us to realise His loving right to us. He so hears our 'Lord, do my will,' that we close with 'Thy will be done,' in a mood which is co-operant much more than resigned. And, after all, if we seek Him for His blessing to us, that is still incipiently theocentric; for it is His will, and not our dream, that He should be thus sought.

But another thing. It may be wrong to transfer the craving frame of mind directly to the larger egoisms, social or patriotic. In our personal religion we begin with God for us. God, by His own will, is for our soul first its redeemer, then its sanctifier into self-forgetfulness. He so saves us from ourselves that some have risen to say they were willing to be lost for His glory. But it may not follow that such anthropocentrism is His providential way for the larger unities, the group-unities whose personality is incomplete. The nations are from the first for God and His Kingdom more than He for them. No nation is an end in itself as a soul is. The idea of a group-personality is a great and fertile one, but it can hardly be allowed to go as far as that. It befits the Church better than the nation, since the Church has what no nation has—a personal Holy Spirit at its core for the permanent source of all its life and change. But we cannot offhand transfer to a people the features or the destinies of the individual soul. We have not, for instance, learned to think of nationality as immortal in the way a soul is immortal.

Nor can we think of it as communing with God like either the soul or the Church. It is not easy to think that God loves the perishable nation in the sense in which He loves either the souls that compose it or the human race it is there to bless. Nor is the nation entitled to the absolute devotion of any soul, since in its history necessity plays, if not a greater part than freedom, yet a part too great for the allegiance of a soul, where freedom takes the lead. Patriotism is not religion. God does not love one nation at the cost of the rest. In His free grace He is for nations only as they are for Him, though He is there for our souls before we are for Him, and as the only means of making us for Him. They are ends in themselves as nations are not. Nations are too impersonal to be the objects of His grace as souls are. They may be His instruments more than His servants, and both more than His friends. They are there for Him more than He for them. A theodicy of history must take this into account, and must not treat national ambitions as sympathetically as those egoist desires which are sound enough for private religion in its beginning. We have, as nations, the right to expect the help of God not as we have a pride of place, but only as we may be of more use than our foes to the Kingdom of God in the world, and not to mere civilisation. In the diplomacy of war it might be an error, stupid and grave, perhaps fatal, that one nation should leave another out of account. But it would be more dense and disastrous still for both to leave out of account the Kingdom of God, and in the policy of States to ignore entirely the principle of the Church.

World calamity bears home to us the light way in which, through a long peace and insulation, we were coming to take the problem of the world, and especially its moral problem. 'We do not now bother about sin' was said with some satisfaction. The preachers protested in vain against that terrible statement—those of them that had not lost their Gospel in their culture. But they were damned with the charge of theology. And now God enters the pulpit, and preaches in His own way by deeds. And His sermons are long and taxing, and they spoil the dinner. Clearly God's problem with the world is much more serious than we dreamed. We are having a revelation of the awful and desperate nature of evil. The task which the Cross has to meet is something much greater than a pacific, domestic, fraternal type of religion allows us to face. Disaster should end dainty and dreamy religion, and give some rest to the winsome Christ and the wooing note. It should discourage a religion more romantic than classic, which sacrifices the institutional truth of faith entirely to its intimate mood, a religion but bland and brotherly, in which the ethical note of justification is smothered in a spurious type of reconciliation. Let us hope that all will result in the discovery of a holier mercy, through judgment braced, and wise by more than pity—by the conquest of the last despair. It is a much wickeder world than our good nature had come to imagine, or our prompt piety to fathom. We see more of the world Christ saw. It calls for a vaster salvation and a diviner Christ than we were sinking to believe. And it must cast us back on resources in that Saviour which the mental levity of comfortable religion, lying back for a warm bath in its pew, was coming to stigmatise as gratuitous theology. The salvation of the world is a much greater agony and victory than any but the very *élite* of the Church's faith had seen, and it calls for more than a Cross merely kind and sacrificial, or a Gospel but blithe and wise. The object of God in His Gospel is something more than to multiply cases of moral excellence in an atmosphere of spiritual culture; it is to produce a realm of justifying, glorifying faith. That is man's chief end—such a faith working out into a kingdom of love—God justifying man, and man justifying God. And both because of God's justification of Himself and His holy way in the Grace and Cross of Jesus Christ.

That would therefore be a blessing from the heart of curse, which recalled us to the old sense, which many a bad theology can yet rouse, of the superhuman greatness and superhistoric deity of the Saviour of such a world. It is a sense much lost amid all the fresh interest with which modern scholarship has invested His historic life, and the new depth it has found in His words. The new historic greatness of Christ may engross us to the neglect of His eternal glory. And there are moments when, in sympathy with modern ideas and hopes, we understand the deniers of any salvation but too well. We ask ourselves incredulously—some who thought their faith on firm foundations ask—whether, as such wickedness seems impossible to one person, however Satanic, the grasp and control of it, to say nothing of its cure, is not also beyond the personality of a Saviour. But these are only moments. The worst calamity of all is calamity falling on a godless world. To that we need not come. In the seeming failure of a God of order we are cast upon a God of crisis, who is God most chiefly in the chief tragedy of things, and from the nettle of perdition plucks the flower of salvation. The victory in Christ's Cross is greater than that in any possible war. When we groan under the dreadful burden the world bears, and when, at the end of our thought, in despair of all else, we are cast upon hourly prayer to the Holy One whose love has borne the burden of a perverse and warring world since the beginning, and who is 'crucified to its end,' we feel that calamities so awful can be in the hands of no mere man, nor within the compass of a human soul. If Christ were but a choice soul and no more, not the elect Son, we should certainly have to pass Him by to reach a Saviour of the world adequate for the human perdition now revealed as by a last trump. But that would be an end of Christian faith. For to that faith God in Christ has taken the responsibility for the destiny of a world whose evil to His eye is worse than wars can reveal to ours, or all our horror gauge. He has spoken, has come, has acted, has overcome. The modern world lives in that victory, however veiled. We begin and end with a faith, not in Jesus simply but in His world work, not simply in His person but in His person's office, in Him as God's Son and Christ and Redeemer, for good and all, the Conqueror and Saviour of a world worse even than we now see, the slow Regenerator of the administration of his purchased property. We begin with the faith in which our own soul calls Him its Saviour from what seems an infinite and hopeless evil. He delivers us from a sin whose guilt lies on our small soul with a pressure from the reservoir of all the high wickedness of the world. It is not from our moral lapses nor from our individual taint that we are delivered, but from world sin, sin in dominion, sin solidary if not hereditary, yea, from sin which integrates us into a Satanic Kingdom. An event like the war at least aids God's purpose in this, that it shocks and rouses us into some due sense of what evil is, and what a Saviour's task with it is. We need not talk of 'total corruption,' but it is the malign and organised evil of a whole intricate and infected world that has got hold of us in various degrees, an evil from which no culture can free us, to which the apparatus of civilisation itself, when captured, may but give the more power and scope. The present state of things is a revelation (such as never came home to the genial pieties of peace) of this superhuman wickedness of the world, which prophets from time to time declared and doomed, only to be called the Jeremiahs of the hour, its *trouble-fêtes*, and the maligners of human nature in the interest of a dead and dismal theology.

It is impossible that the whole dimensions and heinousness of wickedness, the abysmal perdition of humanity, should be grasped by any created soul. Only the absolutely holy can measure sin or judge it. No individual man has mind enough to grasp the wickedness of a nation, nor heart enough to bewail it—to say nothing of morals enough to master it. None but Christ gauged the sin of Israel. And what are we to say of the sin of the whole race ? No single soul of us escapes from the evil far enough to gauge it, to judge it, and therefore to destroy it. None could remain at the same time so intimate in our conscience as to bear it. No godliest saint, promoted for his spiritual purity and heroism to the highest place a creature could win—no such Adoptionist Messiah could cope with the devilry revealed in the cynical inversion of a whole nation's conscience, and the moral convulsion of a world with no resource but war. He could not deliver a single soul from the racial evil which infects it. And, therefore, we are driven back to before the foundation of the world—to a Redeemer who was *there*, who is deeper and older than His human nature, whose Redemption of the world is only possible because of His part in its creation, who took the responsibility of creating because He knew He possessed the power to redeem and retrieve whatever creation might come to. No created being could save the creation, none who only became a king because he nobly and mightily died, but One alone who died so mightily and finally for the world because He was its holy King. None but a supramundane Christ can cope with such evil as comes home to us now. And what we now realise of evil is but a fraction of what the holy eye has seen, His heart borne, and His redemption engaged since history began.

In the New Testament we can see how the belief in such

a Saviour was forced on Christian experience. We can trace the process by which the Christ who was realised as the soul's Saviour was placed by sacred thought for ever by the Father's side at the very creation of the world. Apostolic faith in its thought carried back the implicates of its vast experience of a final salvation. The organ of the second and greater creation which we do know must have been the organ of the first which we do not—unless we are to believe that between Nature and Grace there was not a miraculous action but an impassable gulf. And we can mark the same process, trend, and venture of holy thought asserting itself in the genius of all the great theologies (however criticisable their precise form) which have expounded the Catholic Church's consciousness of its salvation. The whole celestial greatness and glory assigned by them to a Saviour who left heaven with the free purpose of salvation; all the majesty and radiance of conception in which the mediæval thinker and artist set forth His splendour there; the glorious pictured economy of a heavenly world which creation but reflects—it was all but the expansion, in a continuity backwards, of that same deepest principle and surest sense of the soul's Redemption from a world's evil which cast the mind also forward into visions of an Eternal City of God, and an ineffable Jerusalem descending from above. What I try to say is this, that the human collapse, whose deadly greatness is shown anew to-day in the fall of the Lucifer of nations, in proportion as its madness wrecks humanitarian dreams and the modern apotheosis of man, is calculated to wake anew in the Church the sense, nay the faith, which long ago grew up out of Europe's convulsions and perditions in an empire's fall—the faith of the necessary deity and victorious majesty of any one who undertook to be the Saviour of such a world, and who is realised as the Saviour by the soul enmeshed in it, so realised by a whole Church of such souls. How we should formally conceive of such deity and majesty is a further question. But an 'eternal sin' means an eternal Saviour.

Still another thing comes home from world disaster. I hinted it a little ago. The real root of the calamity spreads through the whole spiritual and moral fabric of a natural Humanity too successful to owe itself to any but itself. It is the doom of an age, of an egoist and competitive age, both in the Old World and in the New, whose profits are beyond all proportion to its outlay, and whose wealth is far more than it can guide. It can rule industry but not success. And, if the curse is in civilisation itself, it is in such religion as it has. The conditions of collapse are conditions that belong to modern progress, through its practical neglect of the Kingdom of God, nay, its practical antagonism to it. For not to own its supremacy is to deny its existence or its right. And upon that civilisation does judgment pass. Militarism is but competition writ large and red. In business competition has not rent society because of the immense qualifications and mitigations it has from social, moral, and religious life. In war these are thrown to the winds. But as matter of fact the root of the war has been even more commercial than military.[1] Is the principle of the war very different from that of a general strike, which would bring society to its knees by sheer impatient force, and which so many avoid only as impolitic and not as immoral? The love of man cannot stand up long, whether in capital or labour, without the love of God with its moral principle and quality; and pity dries up without His holy mercy. An international authority vanishes with the faith of that Kingdom of God which speculations about the future so steadily avoid. The judgment descends on a whole progressive world, whose egoist civilisation had replaced

[1] See the fascinating book by Professor Millioud of Lausanne, *The Ruling Caste and Frenzied Trade in Germany* (Constable).

that Kingdom, and found the Church to be but a by-product of national religion, or but another of the empires, with no international voice. Before the half-century of German preparation there were warnings given by moral seers who were in a position to measure the state of European ethic, religion, and politics, and who saw nothing in front but the awful debacle that has now come. In the Appendix to this chapter I refer to the portentous conclusions appended to Bunsen's *God in History* (1860)—warnings repeated, amplified, and varied to no purpose by many men of genius and preachers of faith, both Catholic and Protestant, from then till now. There has been no such drain on a civilisation since the Roman Empire fell to the barbarians of the North. Out of that flux it was the Church of a great, commanding, and super-national Gospel that came with most gain and good. Is the Church to-day equal to the situation of to-day? In the collapse of the ancient civilisation, it was the Church that saved the world for another. Upon the sack of Rome, I have mentioned, Augustine wrote his *City of God*, and opened a new era which he has not yet ceased to mould. But in the collapse of that new civilisation to-day, what is to save us? Can the Church in its rent condition do it again? What is the International which is to save Humanity from egoist nationalism? Can the statesmen with their devices for future peace? Are these not too much the organisation of our fear? Can Rome? Not with her curialism, fumbling at the moral situation, and 'the successor of Peter even in his betrayal'? Can the national churches? The German seems solid for the Belgian crime and the *Lusitania* 'frightfulness.' Can our free Churches? They do not seem to measure the problem. Byzantinised, Chalcedonised, reformed, rationalised, humanised, divided, everything but remoralised by a regeneration, if not an inversion, of values, is the Church evangelised enough still to make men feel that its gospel of judgment and salvation to the conscience is, for men and nations, the moral secret, the dominant power, the judging principle, the one antiseptic, the renewing energy deepest in history ? Can it save civilisation even if by love's fire ? Can it replace in command a righteous because a holy God ? In a world orgy of brute power, has it everything but moral weight on a world scale ? Do not tell me of the good it is doing among the poor. Where should we be without that ? But to talk like that is to parley with the situation, and to miss the whole issue. Was the Church's Gospel God's last word and work for the world ? It has not won the world's heart ; has it lost the world's conscience ? Has it the word and the heart to beard kings and quell spiritual wickedness in high places ? Let the German Church say.

But let us return to the merits of their case for whom such catastrophes impugn a Providence and destroy a faith. This result, I was suggesting, but brings to light a fatal fallacy in what they have been led to expect by the popular type of religion. The whole habit of leisurely apologetic has had in view an evil too remote, passionless, and unrealised, and a God who, if He was not kindness to man, was no God for him. The young mind has been shaped in religion by influences youthful for a grave situation, too feminine for a history of men, and too motherly to reveal the Father-King. Truly we cannot exaggerate the love of God, if we will take pains to first understand it. But we have been taught to believe only in a beneficent and not in a sovereign God, in a tender God in no sense judge, in an attractive God, more kindly than holy, more lovely than good—the God of the children, or of the evangelist, or of the honourable, successful man with the delightful home, the agreeable circle, and the generous hand—a God whose purpose of love became incredible unless it was pursued by winsome ways, and published in fine and tender discourse. The Saviour must wear soft raiment. If ever He was rough, the less a Saviour He. If He seem austere, that, it is said, is through a religion that buries its own talent and takes to monkish interpretation; if He is exacting, it is due to callous theologians without the platform note and the 'great human heart.' And, if His way with civilisation is judgment, if it is not cloudless sympathy and benediction, it ceases to be of grace. Such a habit of mind, now that the lid is off hell, is suddenly struck from its only perch, feels taken in, and asks if such a world as we see can be the means to a loving end, if it could ever be made to contribute to a Divine Kingdom. It has always been taught to conceive of that Kingdom but as the organisation of men in love more thorough than their present organisation in mutual fear and hate. It has not learned to think of it as the reign of a God whose love is holy at any price. It fears anarchy more than it hallows God. It is not used to first-class crisis. And in its shock it can find no theodicy in the course of history, no conduct of things by God worthy of God—worthy of its kind of God, whose Cross was but a kindly boon to crippled men, and not chiefly an honour done to the Holy Name, and the foundation of the Holy Realm.

They have gone to the wrong source. Where shall we get the idea of what is worthy of God? There can only be one source of such knowledge. It is the final account God gives of Himself. It is no expectation of ours, no presumption in us of what a godlike God would do, no imagination of a God projected from our need. God's account of Himself, of His way with man, and of the purpose He infuses into history, His account of His will, on the scale and depth of the great convulsive judgments, is in Christ and His Cross, or it is nowhere. It is in the Cross which so many are disposed to treat as an incident, or at most an object-lesson, though one falsified by all the stern course of history. The Cross of Christ, with its judgment-grace, its tragic love, its grievous glory, its severe salvation, and its 'finished work,' is God's only self-justification in such a world. But is it not a salvation full and free? Surely. Full of the passion which sets the soul free for Himself. Free? It was of His own will. Hard? Yes, but hardest of all for Him. He took on Himself there more than He ever inflicts; and His infliction from us there He turns into His redemption. The Cross meant more change in God than in man. It was His own Act of changing judgment into mercy, His own miracle. And its first concern was His holy love, not ours. Real and thorough religion is theocentric more than anthropocentric. Thus, you see, the revision of our expectations involves the revision of our Creed. It is impossible even to discuss the theodicy all pine for without the theology so many deride. I shall venture to suggest that a call has come to the Church to set its own house in order, and show some deeper sense of the real moral problem—the problem within God, the problem of judgment as atonement—ere it venture to adjust to the conscience the damaged moral order of the world. It is invited by events to discard light solutions, easy beliefs, and endings merely happy; now to rise above its cowardly dread of depth on the ground that it is obscure; to win from God's answer in Christ at least some profounder sense of the world problem and some higher sense of the one and eternal morality; to put down into their proper place the small empirics and the mild mystics who have never descended into hell and therefore do not know the price of heaven, who never tasted damnation and therefore knew not the authentic taste of grace. Unfortunately, the Church's treatment of her truth has allowed it to come to this, that when we use the only language that fits the moral case of mankind, the language of the New Testament, we are supposed by very many who should know better to be discussing theses and holding a brief for some system of theology, instead of handling the last moral powers of heaven and earth, and setting out the final relations of God's conscience and man's.

A Christian optimism has grown up which had begun (like the social passion for brotherhood without righteousness, or with a righteousness which was only fraternity) to dream of a speedy unity of the Churches without a prime regard to their belief. Especially was it indifferent to any grasp of reconciliation deep and drastic enough to fit the present pandemonium; which is man's last masterpiece in the way of unity, progress, or a sympathetic religion. From the German Church, in particular, there comes a blow fatal to any such speedy hope. But the pagan Byzantinism of the German Church is not the only factor in the unhappy situation. The subjectivism, descending to sentiment, to which, in many quarters, Protestantism generally has sunk, its neglect of objective fact, truth, righteousness, and reality, has much to do with the total situation and the bewilderment it creates. A world convulsion is bound to shatter any faith not founded on a world righteousness for ever secured.

We have been taught, for instance, to trust sacrifice as a divine thing in itself, latent in humanity, with the Cross as no more than its superlative. We have been encouraged to measure our religion by the sacrifice we make instead of the sacrifice we trust, by the love we feel instead of the love we love. And now we are compelled to see the wreck of such a creed, as we mark the sacrifice of German faith to German nationalism, and to deplore the sacrifice of German lives and loves to a German state with morals optional. We are shocked into the perception that even a principle like sacrifice may become 'procuress to the Lords of Hell.' For our humanist optimism, the blow is comparable to that given to philosophic optimism by the earthquake of Lisbon in 1755. That event startled people out of the comfortable view that the general course of the world was an apparatus for the harmonious completion of a rational creation in man as the intelligent summit of nature. It drove them to think in terms of crisis (that is, of Gospel) rather than of process (that is, of law): and it led them to view the movement of things as the sphere for the development of moral personality through its collision with nature rather than its harmony—a collision rising, as in the Cross, to tragedy. The anomalous thing then was not cosmic defects but blights upon the soul's ideals and aspirations, or fates that impede personal development, and even make it practically impossible. We may now be startled into a stage of belief higher still. Are we now being taught to see that the world of nature and of man is there for something else than progress—for eternity; for more than man's purposes and glories, even for more than our moral development as persons? Is there not something greater than personality—the Redemption by which alone such as we may become persons? Are we meant to learn that life is there for the production of a personality saved by unique crisis rather than developed by steady culture, one holy in faith rather than moral in self-achievement? The anomalous thing is then not the outer tragedy of fate but the inner tragedy of guilt, and man's chief end is to be forgiven and redeemed. We may be taught that, if we are to be holy at all, we can be holy in *faith* only, and in faith reared on a tragedy rather than a truce. For, so far as we *see*, the holier the soul is, the more it has against it; and the saints, the more they are set on the Kingdom of God, are of all men most miserable if they look primarily to the moral amelioration of the world.

The Kingdom of God in the world means much more than that. Are we being driven to ask whether the spirit of holiness is not the recognition that man's progress is not the supreme goal of God's action in the world, and to question whether he is even its pivot? We are set to inquire on what principle we could secure, not the continuity of evolution, but the supremacy of God's loving glory, and how we are to avoid a mere sanctified Eudemonism and the passion for having a good time in a decent way. We are bidden to recognise that God's demand on man takes the lead of man's demand on God. And both are overruled by God's demand on God, God's meeting His own demand. And we learn unwillingly that only God's justification of man gives the secret of man's justification of God. The justification at the root of all other is God's self-justification. In a word, there is but one theodicy, and it is the evangelical. For the Gospel has the only universal and eternal ethic in its heart, the true, real, and final moral relation of God and man.

APPENDIX TO CHAPTER I

Bunsen wrote his *God in History* in 1860, and though half a century has antiquated some parts of the book, there are a few theses at its end which are striking in the light of recent events, and which show the prophetic insight of this devout scholar and man of the world:—

'Are we not even now living in the midst of one of the great crises, and perhaps on the very eve of a catastrophe of the whole of European society.'

'As to Church matters, neither in doctrine nor in cultus do the formulas now in use correspond to the religious consciousness of the present age.'

'The Church of the future must be recognised as the depository of the root idea of all worship—sacrifice.'

'The political becomes a religious and ecclesiastical crisis, and the ecclesiastical a political. [The political and moral condition of Germany, of which he was chiefly thinking, is the judgment on the Byzantinism which has killed the prophetic voice of its Church.] But what the people and the States really need is an inward moral renewal.'

'The people are demanding from their Governments greater liberty; the Governments are demanding from the peoples greater sacrifices. But few draw the right conclusion from this fact, namely, the existence of an intrinsic contradiction which cannot fail to issue in a World-Crisis.'

'The great Catastrophe now impending will, like all preceding catastrophes, be a Day of Judgment for the World; but it will be followed by a greater and more glorious unfolding of the Kingdom of God.'

'According to the New Testament the design and effect of the second coming of Christ to judgment is to be the founding of a universal Kingdom of God. But if this second coming is to be the sign of conflict and judgment, and therefore of the overthrow of those institutions in Church and State which are so contrary to God, has not Christ already returned? Are we not now living in His presence as the judge who was to come? Which deceive themselves more—the Jews who are still waiting for their Messiah, or the Christians (princes and people) who fail to discern that the Messiah in whom they believe, the Spirit of Judgment, of the Father and the Son, has verily returned to sit in judgment on this thankless and rebellious world?'

'The restitution of all things, therefore, the victory of Christ's Good upon this Earth, is the final Goal of all History.'

'A time will come when an absolute Government in the State will be held to be no less monstrous than a system of slavery. And it will be acknowledged by both parties that Absolutism like Slavery is an even greater misfortune for those who exercise it than for those who obey it.'

'If a divine order of the world exists and is embodied in Jesus, there must come a time when the levying of war will be treated as a relic of barbarism, both irrational and immoral; and any incitement thereto will be regarded as a common crime against all.'

'What fools and knaves they must be who believe that by any arts they can stave off the coming day of retribution.'

Progress, Bunsen would tell us, is measured by Eternity. That is the real standard of what is progress or not. Belief in it is a *faith* and not an induction. All rests on a great central decision as to human destiny, a crucial act and last judgment of God, which took place in Christ. You cannot trace a providence inductively, nor scientifically prove it. Providence cannot be proved from the course of history, only trusted from the positive revelation at certain crises, and at one centrally.

CHAPTER II

THE PROBLEMS: REVELATION AND TELEOLOGY

THE radical questions of a belief are forced upon us anew by each crisis of the world. And the first task of the Church, before it go to work on the situation that a crisis leaves behind, is to secure the truth and certainty for its own soul of its faith in the overcoming of evil by good; an operation which may mean the recasting of much current and favourite belief. Is there a divine government of such a world, a world whose history streams with so much blood, ruin, and misery as to make civilisation seem to many doubtfully worth while? That question means for its answer another, Is there a divine goal of the world? Because, if there is, God who secures it has the right to appoint both its times and its means; and a good government of the world is what helps best in our circumstances to bring us there. But is there such a goal, and where do we find it? How shall we be sure of it? Are we to believe in it only if we can sketch its economy, and trace the convergence of all lines, whatever their crook or curve, to that point? Do I believe that all *is* well with my soul only in so far as I see that all *goes* well? Can we be sure that all is well with the world only if the stream of its history run through no dreadful caves, nor shoot wild cataracts, nor ever sink to a trickle in the sand of deserts horrible? Is there, in spite of all appearance, a divine teleology for the soul and for the race? The evolutionists seem driven more and more to a teleology of the world. Is it a divine one, found in the moral soul and in its eternal destiny for the image of God ?

These, I have said, are questions which it is the business of a practical religion to answer—or, more exactly, of the revelation which is the heart and source of such religion. A revelation will be great, universal, and final just as it does answer such questions, and pacifies even the soul it does not yet satisfy. 'What I do, thou knowest not now, but thou shalt know hereafter.'

We may, perhaps, assume that few in this country cherish a deliberate and reasoned Pessimism as their theology of No-God. Few make Chaos king, or hold disorder to be the original and ideal state of being, whose *faux pas* produced the world and blundered on soul. If they were more logical and radical, perhaps they would develop an explicit creed of this kind, as Germany has, who is now doing her missionary best to restore the world to that first estate. But they do not. They cannot help believing, like the rest of us, in order beneath disorder, within crisis, and over crime. And it is no order merely static. It is a dynamic order that science and experience reveal, not an ordered but an ordering energy, an *ordo ordinans*. Our thought is a mode of action, our action is not a mode of thought. Thought is not thought which merely broods. The order means movement. And it means result. It is no kaleidoscope. It is movement which is not merely interplay, like that of wild creatures restless in a cage, or fish sporting in the sea and making for nowhere. However we modify the idea of evolution, it has defined the movement of things as a swelling procession, and not a mere interaction. Nature not only exists, nor only changes; it grows. It certainly grows in complexity. It grows, with all its order, more heterogeneous. It is full of new departures. It grows in quantity and variety. But does it grow in quality ? Is the evolution really progress ? Is the complexity more than complicated, is it sublimated ? Is it all but a mode of motion, or does the long series rise to action ? Is it really dramatic, or only spectacular ? Is it a play or a tableau ? Does it work up to anything ? Does it work anything out ? Has it a denouement, a reconciliation ? We used to delight in a teleology of its clockwork parts—till their dysteleology, their wryness, got hold of us, till life took the place of scheme, till the watch ticking on the shore gave way to the worm creeping in the sod, the engine to the organism, mechanism to biology. Is there a teleology of nature's living history ? Is there a growing organism of organisms from the mollusk to the man ? And if it come to a head in man, does man come to a head in anything ? He *is* an end—*has* he an end ? Has he a chief end, a destiny ? How do you know ? What is it, where, when ? Does the human history in which nature issues crown the teleological side of nature or the dysteleological, the fitness of things or their 'cussedness' ? Does it seal the order or the ravage of nature ? Does war exist for peace, or peace for war ? Which element is the natural selection of history ? Is there a drift in all things ? And is it a torrent over Niagara, or a fine vapour steaming, like praise, to the hills and the heavens ? Is the world a whole ? And, if it is, is it a whole marmoreal, statuesque, and symmetrical, or organic, vital, and moving. If it move, what is its goal ? Has it a perfection, and is that perfection in itself ?

Such are the questions that a world calamity brings home in passionate and tragic terms. Perhaps, if we survey them in our calm, we may find an anchorage ready in our storm. Through the clearer water we may discern a bottom that will hold when our old moorings drag.

Are you clear what the questions are ?

Creation means life, movement, evolution. What is the goal and where ? We cannot see it simply by looking out. The future is a book shut and sealed. The great end does not gleam, a City of God with shining towers, on the horizon that closes our gaze. Can we, then, presume it from a survey of history as far as it has gone ? Can we calculate the final trend, if we do not see the point of convergence ? How can we ? How do we know how much of history is yet to run ? Is the decisive part, the fifth act, yet to come ? Have we any idea in which act we entered the house ? We see but a small area of all time as yet. And the lines are neither straight, nor on any calculable curve. They are labyrinthine. The Ideal offers us at best but an asymptotism, always closing never meeting, which makes a certain irony for progress and freedom—perpetual approximation mocked by perpetual severance, eternal passion, and eternal pain. We go forward sure of something which is uncertain, or, at least, ever unattained. The soul craves a goal, and the goal mocks the soul. The soul is a whole, a unity. The very pain of its inner strife witnesses to that. It is the only unity we seem directly to know. Has it a perfection ? Will its strife depart in peace and a fullness of days ? Is the perfecting of that personal unity its destiny, or shall its warfare at a stage dissolve it to dust ? The soul's own instinct is to go on. But God has set a concern for the world in our heart. Has the world a unity and a destiny corresponding to the instinct of the soul and to its resentment of dissolution ? From the course and curve of history it is hard to say.

But, if the destiny of the world is to be reached by no induction from its history, or any part of its history (such as the modern world), is history therefore only dumb ? Or shall we find at some point of crisis a significance we miss in the long lines of career ? What is that point ?

Ourselves, our hearts? Shall we trust the echo or the intuition in our own heart and its sympathies? But how unsteady! How individual! How inadequate for history as a whole, to say nothing of the finality of Eternity! Can the Eternal become historic? History at large may be personalistic (as the conception of the group-personality in societies shows), but is it, is Humanity, a personality in any such sense as would permit it to be the vehicle for the revelation of a personal God? And were history equal to the utterance, is the Eternal capable of such self-expression? Is there any historic spot where Eternity affirms in a person the impressions of an hour, where we are given what we cannot reach, and given it on the world scale and for ever? What we cannot achieve, do we receive, and receive in advance as the achievement of another? Is there any spot where the whole world has already come to a head, and God has come to His own? Does the God of the world emerge as final anywhere within it? Is there any soul which is for history the visitation of Eternity? Have we any assurance in history that it has not only an order and course but a final principle and value? Has it a meaning behind all the plexus of law and cause that we can trace in it? Is it a transparency with its light beyond, or only a scheme in black-and-white? Has it a worth beyond any system of it? Is it expressive or stolid? Has it a symbolism? Is it a sacrament? Does it speak beyond itself, and present its events in more than a train of sequence? Is the past but a sky of formal constellations, or is it in a grand conspiracy of eloquence and action? Does it offer anything beyond the sight of science to the insight of soul? If it do, what is it? Is it but the vague suggestions that open to the poet, or the moral monitions carried to the prophet? If it go beyond Buckle, does it stop upon Carlyle? Is even insight all we can reach—spiritual penetration and grand surmise? Do we come but to trust for the world our best instincts enlarged? Is religion but such insight? Is it but a fresh interpretation of life by genius? If it is no more, is it not then the monopoly of genius, or at least of temperament? Have we left for real revelation a place of its own and a function of its own for true, universal faith, the faith of the ungifted man? Is apostolate but a mode of genius? Is faith but instinct's greatest and surest intuition? Or in revelation have we a real gift, 'a synthetic judgment'? And in faith have we a departure as great and new as genius, and as much higher than genius as when genius rose from common sense? Is there, creating faith at a historic point, something which settled all else in an eternal crisis and conquest, and which is yet in such an organic context with the word that it gives meaning and certainty to all? Have we there the search-light of the world, that not only gleams forth through the transparency of things, but sees into us far more powerfully than we see into it, and does for us what we can never do for it? Beyond its symbolism which *shows*, is there anywhere the kind of revelation that *acts*, that searches, and, beyond searching, gives, and, beyond giving, decides and creates? Is there any divine visitation that puts us in possession, *in petto*, of the goal of all surmise? Is there any divine gift and deed that fixes the colours seen by genius in the eternal purpose and Kingdom of God, where all earth's hues are not mere tints but jewels —not mere purpureal gleams, but enduring, precious foundation-stones?

To all such questions Christianity answers with an everlasting yea, however Christendom may blur or belie it. The eternal finality has become a historic event. There is a point of Time at which Time is no longer, and it passes into pure but concrete Eternity. That point is

Christ. In Christ there is a spot where we are known far more than we know. There is a place where God not only speaks but comes, and not only vouches but gives, and gives not only Himself to the soul, but, by a vast crisis, the soul to itself and the world to His Son. Our error and uncertainty go back at last for their power to our guilt, and they pass away in the gift of the grace that destroys it. The grace that magnifies the guilt in the act of mastering it takes away the doubt. Trust gives us the security denied to sight. We escape from evidences to realities. Our dreams of good become the certainty of God. In Christ God is not preached but present, and not only kind but mighty, not only willing but initiative, creative. He does more than justify faith, He creates it. It is His more than ours. We believe because He makes us believe—with a moral compulsion, an invasion and capture of us. He becomes our eternal life. To live is Christ. He is our destiny. He is our career. And He is the same yesterday and for ever. The soul's goal is always the soul's God. The world's perpetual destiny is the world's Eternal Redeemer. We inherit 'a finished work.' We receive, in advance, the end of our faith, which is the salvation of our souls in the salvation of a world. We receive, in the *Holy* Spirit (the Spirit of a perfection which is always completely its own end), the pledge and instalment of our common heritage. This talk is scriptural in phrase, but it is not antiquated in sense—except as we may have come so to regard the whole miracle of the Spirit, who is always changing Time into Eternity, and turning the Christ of the past into the soul's real present. We possess, in a living and present Christ, God's goal and destiny of the soul and of the world. We are put (miraculously, it is true, by the Spirit) in possession of a God whose holy self-sufficiency secures the certainty of His purpose, and whose purpose is the world's salvation to Himself in a kingdom. It is not a salvation to prosperity, nor to civilisation, nor to idealism, but to Himself, to His obedience, His communion, His realm. In this revelation the economy of salvation becomes the principle of the movement of the universe. Nature is but a draft scheme of salvation with the key on another sheet, where the eternal act of redemption is found to carry and crown the long process of creation. It is God's salvation of the world that dominates the long history of the world—infallibly, if not at every point palpably. Such is the position of Christian faith, and it is the ground of all our good hope and sure outlook for the future. Such is the nature of Christian teleology. It rises from our experience of the Christian revelation.

The more recent trend of the philosophy of history points this way. The temptation is strong for many to-day to construe life on a scheme of evolution borrowed from the natural world, and passing through the normal points of birth, bloom, and death. But we are arrested in this scheme by several facts when we are dealing with personal life. For instance, the beginning of that life is not with birth, but with the first exercise of the soul in an act of free choice. Then its development does not lie in natural process, but in a series of such acts of choice, in which the personality asserts itself against the processes that would but hurry it, as a thing, down a stream. Its culmination, again, is not mere blossom, it is not in the easy, unconscious play of forces, but in the deliberate harmony of the self-asserting will with an ideal conceived, pursued, and more or less attained. And finally, death is not simply failure as blameless decay, but it is bound up with a failure with which we charge ourselves; and our best life is a gift in the midst of such failure, a gift of mercy, forgiveness, redemption, eternity.

When we pass from life as merely organic to life as

personal, we have to do with something more than mere movement; it is more even than mere evolution from simple to complex, from coarse to fine. We have to do with a history. And what is a history (if we begin with the personal history we know best) but a movement in which an inner something that abides is always being translated into a changing career more weighty and more wide. The Eternal becomes Time without ceasing to be Eternity. The timeless becomes historic, by a process which is the root of all miracle. We are even more concerned with the inner identity than with the outer variation, with the reality than with its appearance, with the power than with the plexus in which it expands, with the person than with the career. It is this permanent personal element that is not in nature. It is this spiritual that is the eternal. Souls last longer than systems. Now history, in the large impersonal sense, is a system by comparison with a soul. But yet even that history is not a mere evolution, not a mere series of phases, not a mere chain of phenomena. It is the evolution of something. It is something evolving. And it is an evolution that does not go on in the way of nature, merely as a deeper complication and finer interaction of phenomena. The introduction of the idea of the group-personality into history brings with it that action I have named of translation, the translation of an inner power into an outer phase. The form in which the onward movement takes place is a series, not of phases, but of something far more—of decisions more or less free by an inner soul and will, self-assertions of the thing that abides. This is the feature of personality; and though it cannot be applied to history as a whole offhand, though humanity is not a great person, yet it holds of personality so far as that the great personalities are its great agents. When we are speaking of personal growth, therefore, and indeed of history altogether, whether individual or corporate, as distinct from the evolutionary pomp, we are in another category than natural process. We have not only a difference from nature, we have a reversal of nature; for our choice can go back on nature's process. It is nature taken in hand by an inner power, with a freedom above nature. Thus the notion is not one of life blooming and then fading, with a vital rise and a dying fall. Life has what has been called a dramatic character. Will is involved in it—choice, conscience, reason, and action. It is a movement, a crescendo, of moral action, and not of natural process. Nay, it is further said, and with poignant truth, that it is, in most cases, not dramatic simply but tragic. But it is tragic in a deeper than the outward, obvious, and impressive sense. It is not the tragedy of an external fate falling on the inner will. It is the tragedy of the inner will itself falling. It is the man's own fall, and not the fall of his fortunes. It is his moral tragedy, the fall not from happiness but from holiness—the tragedy not simply of gloom but of guilt. Behind all the tragedies of incident lies the tragedy of guilt. And the supreme theodicy is that which adjusts with the goodness of God not the appalling catastrophes men suffer, but the less striking, though more paralysing, tragedy of what they have done and become.

This is a line of thought which is forced upon us as soon as we begin to give the individual his due value in the system of things or ideas. The ideal construction of history, which came to a head in the impressive architecture of Hegelianism, fell and broke upon the new sense in the nineteenth century of the value of the individual. And not only on his value in the sense of his preciousness, but in the sense of his power, the sense of him as a creative, invasive, deflective, incalculable power. In Hegel's system there is no room left for such an individual, and that was the defect that brought down its grand flight. A closer and more scientific treatment of history showed that ideas have been effective only as they passed through the thought of individual personalities, and were stamped or driven by their will. The general lines, the great features, the imperial ideas of history were not all, nor even most. Taken alone, they bleached all the complexion out of history, and left but a pale form, moving but anæmic. They had a far more vital and organic connection with their personal agents than Hegel allowed; these were not mere wires on which the ideas travelled nor vortices where they met. Man was made a living soul by a life-giving Spirit, he was not the pawn of a moving process even of thought.

What did this change mean from our point of view? It meant that the key of history was to be sought in the will as free and not as the puppet of ideas nor as a vortex of force. It lay in a soul and not in a system. It was found by faith in a soul and not by sight of a scheme. If the individual is a synthesis of influences and directives, he is yet not a mere resultant. He is what Wundt calls 'a creative synthesis.' He is not simply a crossing point nor a point of fusion; he contributes. He gives as truly as he receives, and if he do not give he ceases to receive. He brings to the ideas round him something more than they supply. There is a miraculous something in him as effect which is not in them as cause. He is himself a directive. There is in the man a reacting, and controlling, and constructing power over the influences that produced him. And in that element lies the key of history. Thought has turned from tracing the drift in a whole to trusting the gift in a soul. It has turned from speculation to revelation, from revelation as truth to revelation as Person, from the certainty of induction to that of inspiration, from synthesis to intuition, from laws to powers, from the revelation in order to the redemption in crisis, from the social order to social catastrophe, judgment, and regeneration. Interest has passed from the classic to the romantic, from the symmetry of ubiquitous evolution in history to the broken eloquence of its symbolism, from its system to its meaning, from historical constructions to historical values. The constellations of affairs rain influence down. We turn from the mere march of events to their formative goal, and its incessant reaction upon their course. We are led by a light and power that beats back on us.

The permanent thing, therefore, which makes movement history, and corresponds to the ego in the changing man, is not a *grand être* suffusing the historic career in a monistic way; but it is a living person acting (at a lower stage) like the Holy Spirit which makes an association a church. It is there, in that person, that we have the purpose not of history only but of creation. All the world is a means, and its fashion passes away; but the soul is its end and that abides for ever. All is but machinery just meant to give a bent to the soul; God and the soul endure. The centre and goal of things is where the soul of God and the soul of man completely meet, not in mere rapture but in action. But in this region facts cease to be things and become persons and events. And if this centre is a fact and not a mere ideal, it is a historic and personal fact. It is Christ. The revelation, and, therefore, the justification, of God is not to be found in a visible convergence of all things upon a perfectly happy state, but in the eternal meaning and action of a perfectly holy soul in the profoundest human crisis. It lies in His action upon the soul's relations, especially with God, and upon the dramatic, tragic course of affairs. The final theodicy is in no discovered system, no revealed plan, but in an effected redemption. It is not in the grasp of ideas, nor in the adjustment of events, but in the destruction of guilt and the taking away of the sin of the world. Behind the tragedy of fate to man's happiness, I have said, is the will's tragedy to God's holiness, the tragedy of guilt. And a God who can deal in mercy with that has fully in hand, at the long last, the misery and mystery of man's fate. The agony in the garden heals all the agony of the race.

That is to say, for Christian faith, there is a sure goal of the world, and a controlling teleology thereto; which is not only indicated, as a poet's great surmise, nor only announced as a prophet's burthen, but is given in Christianity as a God-accomplished fact, as the new creation, the Reconciliation. The gift is the world's new birth in pain, not its happy rehabilitation. It is the Reconciliation, and not simply the means to come by it. The Cross is not the machinery of it but the exercise of it, its action not its preliminary. Behind the first creation God was always the new Creator. The final reconciliation is always in God's possession ('Son, Thou art ever with Me'); and, by His gift in Christ, it becomes a possession of ours as we are in Christ. The ruling passion of our moral person for perfection receives its consummation there—in that crisis of cosmic regeneration. We come to ourselves in the soul-certainty of faith, which believes that the world is the work, the end, and the trophy of a perfectly Holy God, and that it is therefore for him already perfect in His Son, it is already a saved whole. And, in the same act and paradox of faith, we know that our souls, though so deeply involved in the vast world, are at the same time also microcosmic wholes. They are involved in it in such a way as still to be ends in their social selves, and not merely means to a social whole. We seize the paradox, so vital to religious experience, of a Whole of wholes, a paradox which can only be expounded by a philosophy of personality with its unique power of interpenetration, mutual involution, and reciprocal indwelling.

That is to say, there is a teleology of the whole world,

but it is only for Christian faith—only in virtue of the salvation of a world in which each soul is worth more than a world without soul. It is quite absurd and quite indubitable. The only possible teleology is an evangelical. It is of grace and faith on an imaginative scale. To use the language of theology, it is a teleology only guaranteed by a soteriology. The only perfection is in salvation. We are born not to prosper but to be redeemed. The unity of the race is only sure in its goal, and that is its redemption. It is the unity of a world of personal ends reborn. We believe in a great destiny for the world because we have a faith in its redemption which rests on the experience of our own, but is no mere expansion of it. We believe in human nature by a faith neither in its excellence, its prosperity, nor its civilisation; in the strength neither of an apparent trend to amelioration, nor of a growing consecration of happiness, nor of an ideal glorification of Humanity; but as a result of our living faith in the world's Redeemer and His Redemption. That is the only teleology of the world which is as sure as sorrow, death, the soul, or its God. Of course it is theological religion. A religion without a theology can never be a world religion. It cannot assure the world of a future.

There was an occasion when Christ was asked a question of theological curiosity—if the goal of salvation would include few or many. And His answer, nationally viewed, was disappointing—as if for Him such an inquiry was academic, or only inquisitive. He converted it at once into a religious occasion. He turned it into the central and primary theology, where we are not merely curious but concerned. He said that such inquiries could only be solved practically, only if a greater question were first settled for our own soul; that eschatology was a matter of soteriology, and soteriology a matter of personal salvation; that we had no key to the eternal future of others except what we had for our own; that our interest in the saving of the world might be perverted to submerge our own salvation; that, in the desire to know, or even in our haste to effect, the destiny of the race, we might miss in our soul the certainty which was the root of all other. 'Are the saved few?' 'Few enough to make you afraid you may not be there. See to your entry. The religious inquisitives may be eternal failures. So may the religious bustlers. You must taste salvation to discuss it. You must experience the world's salvation to deal with the saving of the world' (Luke xiii. 23). As if He should say: 'Acquaint yourself with what God has done. Immerse yourself in it. The consummation will not come by man's gradual organisation under a law of love, but by the consummating Act and Gift of God in His Kingdom and its righteousness—by that and each man's part in it.'

But that Act it was far from easy to take home. Grace is free but not easy. It was not in the growth of man's delectable breadth and charity that Christ found the way to heaven; He cast His inquirers upon a narrow way ending in a strait gate. It was not to a wider knowledge or a larger vision that He looked for the central and final theodicy. The only final theodicy He knew was God's saving Act, in which He Himself grew more and more straitened till it was accomplished. To know and taste that was everything. The world's history did not make for Him the world's final judgment; it worked up to such a judgment, where He is Himself on the bench. Love's straightening for a tangled world was a cure for its sin—it was propitiation, the mercy of the Cross. 'Herein is love—that He gave His Son as propitiation.' Love that meets need finds that to be the chief need. Its first last gift to man is the Cross. This Cross became not only a rescue from a strait but the principle and measure of the whole world. The Lord of the Cross is the final trustee of universal judgment. The whole purpose of history, if we are to believe Christ, was something more than the disentangling of a moral muddle, the evolution of a moral order, or even the growth of a moral personality; it was the redemption of that personality. Its final ethic is that involved in faith with its justifying, regenerating power. It was to bring every man to deal with Him as Saviour, to plant every man at last before the judgment-seat of His Cross and Grace, to work in every man the supreme conviction of belonging to Him, and finding in Him his own new soul—new, yet his own. So that no man comes to himself till he come to Him, and the world does not 'arrive' till it settle to rest in Him. That is the Christian teleology of history, whether we accept it or do not. Christ, judge and justifier, is the one theodicy. The whole race says, 'for me to live is Christ.' Everything exists for Him—love, culture, war, tragedy, glory. He is the one moral touchstone of God and man for ever, the crucial point of the eternal and immutable morality of the Holy.

To believe in a teleology, we must be in possession of the telos. What is called realism is here as useless as what is known as idealism. Any photographic or punctilious reality is, and must always be, incomplete. It is sterile to refer us to facts till we settle the selection of the facts. Only certain facts are fertile. We must have an end to guide our choice. We need the significate to complete the symbol, the meaning to finish the fact. The literary type of realism goes in blinkers—seeing keenly, but only what is under its nose. It does not lift up its head even to look for the reality that closes the vista of its realities. Hence its views oscillate from optimism to pessimism; even in the serious philosophies they do, from the days of Epicurus and Zeno to Hegel and von Hartmann. Hence also it does not pass beyond process to purpose (as the Monism of the day does not). So we must begin with the end, taken as a gift. We must carry it back to the beginning. The purpose is not revealed in the process, but the process in the purpose. That is the guide in our selection and treatment of facts—at least in the moral world. The savage does not explain the saint, but the saint the savage. Creation does not explain Christianity, but Christianity creation. We cannot frame some teleology of life, and then rise from it to a living God who is serviceable to it; but we must descend upon it from that God, from a God otherwise given, self-given, given, therefore, with absolute certainty, and not with a high probability. For He is the end, He does not simply cherish it, and He does not simply declare it, and He does not simply produce it. He *is* our peace. We began in Him in whom we end. We die in our nest. The light of our first sight came from Him who is the object of our last faith. Our great destiny is as certain as He is absolute and holy. But we possess such a God, the Reality of reality, and the Act in all action, only in Christ, the historic Christ on His Cross. Though God is hinted freely in the world, we possess Him securely and finally only in Jesus Christ, the Redeemer, the Redeemer of the conscience, the Holy Redeemer. Who thus masters conscience is King of men. He masters man's inner master. Who masters it by forgiveness is King of Love, of a Holy Love, a moral Eternity, a realm of righteousness. The King of Holy Love is righteous Lord of all the Eternity that we crave or He reveals.

With this security we can sit loosely to many anomalies which seem to rule God out of the course of things. Our faith did not arise from the order of the world; the world's convulsion, therefore, need not destroy it. Rather it rose from the sharpest crisis, the greatest war, the deadliest death, and the deepest grave the world ever knew—in Christ's Cross. We see not yet all things brought under salvation, but we see Jesus the Saviour of all. We taste Him. The Church is not there to exhibit progress and its optimism, but to reveal Christ and His regenerating power. Most of the detail of His working is hidden from us; what He is and does for our own soul is mostly unknown to us; but there is no reality unknown to Him, and no crisis unprovided for, or out of hand. The wisdom of God is the deepest wisdom of the world. It is its latent process (Eph. iii. 9-11; Rom. xvi. 25, 27). The grace of God, with its method, is the ground plan of the universe (unless Christ be a fine failure). All the old creation runs up into it, all the new flows down from it. We do not trace it at every stage of development, but we trust and worship its constant action none the less. The gift to us is not a system of theodicy at work but Holy Love's omnipotence in command. To know Christ's God, as apostles expound His revelation, is to know the long dominants of order and purpose in nature and history. His glory is His majesty, and His majesty is His mercy, and His mercy is by judgment unto holy victory and endless peace. In face of the horrors, moral and physical, around us, and amid all misgivings, that is our faith, our stay, and our last word.

CHAPTER III

METAPHYSIC AND REDEMPTION

SOME are much fascinated by a reasoned Pessimism which seems to them the happy combination of the monistic idea, which is so modern, and the redemptive idea, which is so Christian. And they are led to think that this combination offers, in the region of thought, that reconciliation which is also such a Christian idea. Those who are thus interested are the few probably, and outside of them the rest may find the discussion not only uninteresting but unintelligible. Such may be advised to pass over this chapter, where I wish to return to the previous one, and to the former of the two classes named at its outset.

I will venture to place before me a monist, of the views there described, and I will ask him to follow me from what I take to be a common point of departure, as it might be set forth by a sympathetic thinker like Edward von Hartmann, who keeps moral and spiritual issues well in view, and especially the need of redemption, however pessimistically construed. Let us begin with the recognition of an objective order and of a dreadful breach in it which is fundamentally moral, whether the explanation of the breach be theological or not. Let us then ask this question, Is there in the moral order a self-healing power, as nature overgrows in course of time catastrophes volcanic in violence and in area continental ? Has it a *vis medicatrix*, a power of innate self-recuperation, corresponding to what we find in physical organisms ? Is there in it an indwelling tendency which moves to repair all damage at last, and a power to overbear those elements which arrest its development? Has the moral order this successful power of self-assertion against its foe? Can it carry it to the pitch of self-establishment? Can it at last plant itself on the universe and in command of it? Is the self-assertion not only indomitable as a spirit and tendency, but is it effective, is it irresistible, in the result? Can it secure its own end?

This is a question which resolves itself into another. I have just spoken of the end. Is that end only something far off? Is the path to it only tentative? What is a real means? Do the movements toward the end only peer and grope? Do they only stumble about, feeling this way and that with awful tentacles and experiments, till one of them happen to light upon the end? Have we any security that one ever will light upon it? Or is it rather thus? Is the end already there, deeply there and working itself out? Is it deeply and dominantly imbedded in the whole process, forming a permanent touchstone there for a true means, and refusing all false avenues by a native flair? Is there always within the moral order, however eclipsed, the active immanence of its own end, its own goal?

So long as it is not a question of a conscious immanence our monist friend would probably say, Yes, if he were of the ethical breed and spiritual sensibility of which I have named von Hartmann as a fine example. But there is a third alternative. The end, however immanent, may be, still more deeply, a given thing, a donation rather than a product, a redemption rather than a recuperation. Is it certain whether the recovery is a native reaction in the moral order or an importation into it from something more than a moral order, from personality? and if it be imported is it imported as a reality by the power of a divine personality, or merely as a construction by the imperious habit of our personality? Is it God's recovery or our discovery? If we think of this order monistically, simply as the active νόμος, or norm, or uniform behaviour of a universal substance, have we more to go on than a presumption or an impression when we cherish a faith in its final reign? Will things end where they seem to tend? Has law its own guarantee of finality? Regulative law, organising, punitive law, has little of a saving element in itself. Mere order, with all its uniformity or consistency, need not be eternal. Mere pressure need not be permanent. There may one day be an outleap of hidden fires which are quite unknown or unsuspected now, and which make all known pressures fly. The decisive thing is not in law but in that force behind law. Is that control calculable? Is it certain by any means, whether calculable or not? Can it be relied on? Well, if it can neither be trusted nor got at, faith is impossible. It is only when we find in movement and its law more than law, only when we discover a control of control, that our faith and hope rise as to the future. And for the conviction of eternal permanence and victory we must realise that always behind and within the empirical νόμος there is the ideal but potent τέλος—whose end is always in itself. The great, final, and absolute reality is immanently and urgently coming to itself in all the ordered action of the hour.

But now what is the nature of that reality which besets us before and behind, that end which not only waits for us but works in us, and works especially in the way of repair, redemption, and reconciliation? What is the nature of an end that can realise itself in the face of all opposition? This is a question which makes some demand on philosophical thought, not to say metaphysical language. The object of philosophy is totality. It lives in the whole. It works with wholes. It regards the absolute, the fundamental, final whole in everything. While the Philistines laugh an accomplished writer in *The Times*, just as I pen these words, analyses laughter itself into a mode of our inextinguishable intuition of the absolute which thus besets us before and behind, and is in our best nonsense its real charm. All this casts us upon a metaphysic. We can no longer rest content with philosophic Agnosticism. Metaphysic is the philosophy of totality. But we have now gone further. We have passed beyond a metaphysic of mere rarefied substance for that totality, what might be called the metaphysic of obvious and amateur pantheism. This handles only a totality of mere pervasive but static being—a universal. But a universal is not the same as a whole; it is only a factor of the whole. It may be, like the ether, a very thin universal without the content and wealth of a whole. But we go further still. Besides escaping from mere substance, we pass beyond the notion of a totality of *thought*. Pure thought, however encyclopædic, however universal, cannot cope with the wealth of the whole; were it as architectonic as Hegel's, it cannot. It is not dynamic, not creative, enough. It is not full enough. What we have to do with is not the kind of fullness represented by saturated being, nor even being which is self-organising, self-consistent, and self-contained. It is not fundamental thought we have to do with but fundamental *energy*, which has power not simply to pose its opposite, the inert, but to transform it continually into the energetic. The fullness of the whole earth is a fullness flushed and glorious in power. An ontological metaphysic is replaced by a metaphysic of energy, whose business is to develop the notion not of an abstract universal, but of a concrete totality, a living, rich, and inexhaustible whole, a fullness of power and life. New theories and hypotheses are to be rated not by how they look but by what they can do; not by their skill of ranging themselves in the good society of systems, but by their power to work, and to work initiatively—not simply to be effective but to be creative. The one God is He who makes the new man.

But, when we come to energy and action, can we stop there? Can we stop short of the supreme kind of action which we call an act, a moral act? The moral interest remains uppermost, where it was when we started with the moral order; but we pass now from moral order to moral action. That is more than mere vitality, force, or movement on certain lines of law guiding conduct. We describe movement as moral for other reasons than because it works well and smoothly for the harmony of a system or the happiness of a group. That need not carry us beyond mere utility. We mean the kind of movement possible only to a personality; we mean moral action, action carrying the stamp of that personality and revealing it. We mean movement which not only makes for an end but for an end it selects, and selects for reasons drawn from its own nature, selects, therefore, by a *moral* necessity; it is movement that makes for an end of purpose, and one to which it has power to bend other movements or things. This is the kind of energy of which we are most conscious, the only kind we truly and intimately realise—the energy of ourselves—the energy we *are*. We therefore pass from energetic idealism to personal idealism. And, if we are not to stick in Solipsism, we construe the universe in terms of its crowning product, soul, conscience, and society. It exists for the growing of personality which is an end in itself, and, in so far as it serves, it serves only another personality, and grows men of God, who is the end for all ends. Among personalities (when we pass beyond the dear) we are interested chiefly in the classic, and above all, the providential personalities. And among these above all is that One who has His universal end completely in Himself, who is identical with the end of the disordered universe — with its redemption. He is *the* Redeemer because He is identical with His own redemption.

The last reality, when reality is so understood, so morally and personally, is the Holy. The moral order of society has the absolute morality, the Holy, working almightily in it. That is to say, the supreme interest of society is not progress but the moral eternity active in every stage of progress, and mighty to redeem its regress. It is not progress, but that complete, absolute, unprogressive reality, which is both source, impulse, and law for all progress, and which tests every movement as progress by the extent to which it gives active, holy reality effect. Progress itself is left behind by this interest. It ceases to ride men like an incubus or a fate when they are really concerned about eternity. And nothing is progress which does not carry home our freedom from it, the emancipation from it of those who once thought we could be made free by it and it alone. The root of all progress is redemption and regeneration by the Holy, the Eternal.

Where shall we find the providential reality then? Surely where we find in history the holy and its finality. Surely in the region of energetic, that is to say experimental, religion—in Christ. Not in religious thought, nor in moral action of the more outward and pedestrian sort, but in the morality which we feel working most mightily in the sanctifying grace that rescues, rules, and shapes our inmost life as a race; in morality of the grand style —in justification; in Redemption, as not only a new departure but a new creation, in the morality of the new birth and the new righteousness which make us really men of God. We turn to the moral energy whose righteousness transcends all distributive justice, and which is known by us as the foundation, redemption, and destiny of the world because it is the grace and providence we find at work founding our own moral life and destiny by a revolution at the innermost. For that salvation of ours comes to us in the salvation of a world, and not of our own soul single and alone. The same Act saves both. We do not find our freedom and peace merely by finding ourselves, but by finding ourselves in a world Saviour. We do not reach rest merely by finding our place in an objective order, and reconciling ourselves to it. For that is rather resignation than reconciliation. What we find is a power rather than a place, a power working congenially in us both to will and to do. We do not merely win a fortitude which accepts our niche in the universe, or takes the room assigned in the caravanserai of life. We recognise, especially in the social law, and most especially in the society of the Church, our own Master's voice, the voice of One whose mastery of us is our own true self, true power, and true freedom. *Qui amavit novit quid haec vox clamat.*

Moral power is, at the last, personality. That is the only form in which we know what power really is—our own sense of acting as persons, or of being acted on by persons. There is no possibility of translating νόμος to τέλος, law into destiny, pressure into promise, order into perfection, except by a τέλος or goal whose personality is the immanent ground of the νόμος. It is as a person that the end works within the course, and 'arrives.' It is by the ultimacy, within the course, of a Will absolute and holy, forming the ground and measure of every relative stage. Is there any other category but that of creative personality which makes it possible to conceive of the end already present and active in the means, and realising itself there? The moral order is self-repairing only in the sense that it is repaired continuously and creatively by the Holy One whose end is in Himself, and who is its true self and more. (So that to love God is to love ourselves in the truest way.) That the continuity and stability of the whole moral order is really the unity of a holy Person on that scale is the historic witness of the best and holiest of the race. And it is a serious thing to differ with the saints. Moreover the transcendent ground, immanent and emerging in all things, passes, at its summit in Humanity, into the ethic of personal relations. How then can it be other than personal ? How can it be thus ethical in its results if it is not ethical in its nature—ethical, that is, in the sense of being a personal act of a holy kind, and not only a movement of tendency to a harmony of parts in a utilitarian way. It must be moved by a moral act, by the act of a person on that scale, and not by a non-moral process, if it is to have really moral effect.

So, if we end with the question with which we began as to the self-recuperative power of the moral order, we have found in answer that physical analogies are not enough. For they are all limited. There comes a point when the power of physical self-repair ceases—in death. So that only our own experience in that moral order can be a guide to us. No analogy, no outer observation can. But such experience is more than introspection. It becomes a matter of history. It means not sinking into ourselves, but scrutinising the facts of history, *i.e.* the personalities with the relevant and classic experience. For the greatest matters it is more fruitful to interrogate the classic souls than to circularise the average man. These souls form the locus of authority about the ultimate action and resource in the moral order. But then as a fact the weightier part of the human history they inhabit and interpret has transpired under the faith, not simply of a redemptive process, but of a holy, personal Redeemer. It has been lived out as the action of that Holy One replacing (so far as that is morally possible) the action proper to the soul concerned. We all inherit the legacy of such an ethos. It is impossible now for us to get at any experience relevant to our question from which that historic action is erased. We cannot go back upon history, cast off all that Christian faith has made us, and examine a moral order *per se*, drained of the action of Christian Redemption. The result would be a mere abstraction. And to explain the Christian Redemption as itself the classic case of a self-recuperative moral order is to beg the question. Where is the moral order found whose independent scrutiny yields the critical principle for the interpretation of Christianity ?

A tendency to self-recuperation we *may* find in such order or process as we can reach in nature apart from Redemption, but not a power, a certainty, a finality. We may see that there is in evil an immanent dialectic by which it disorganises itself as evil, that it is a self-solvent, that wickedness tends to destroy the personality that works wickedness, that the bad are caught in their own net, and even that they are made to work out a good they never meant, and on the whole do what they strove to undo. But that perception, even when taken together with certain signs of amelioration, is not the same as the final certainty of the establishment of good in command of the world. We can have that only in the Holy One, and in His self-revelation in supreme action as the Redeemer of the history in which He appears.

Be it remembered that we are not dealing with a mere *élan*, nor a mere *nisus* in a certain direction. The action of the moral upon us is not a case of pressure but of imperative. It is not the flush and tide of a universal wave, making its slow and ebbless way through creation, with power to hold what it covers. It does not act by force but by authority. It is the Whole acting, not by virtue of its mass or energy, but by its right. When the moral acts with universal and absolute right, it is the Holy. And, when it is resisted, the resistance is not simply to be overborne and erased; it must be converted and recovered, else the Holy is less than universal, infinite, and absolute. The unholy must be restored to holiness. It is unmade but to be remade. And there is none but the Holy creative enough to do this. And He must—by the necessity of His holiness. The same Holy who is imperative as law is also creative as life; He is creative and restorative by a necessity moral and not physical, of impulse and not pressure. The power that condemns is the only one that can reclaim. He even atones. As holy He deals with His broken law in the Act which heals the broken soul. The Holy One is the atoning Redeemer. And the source of our moral fear is the goal of our holy love.

No evolutionary process, therefore, can deal justly with the moral situation of the race but only a holy and redemptive. And its redemptive treatment is no mere process but a moral Act. It is the supreme case of that which marks moral action with its fresh initiative and new contribution—it is creative. If any man come to be in Christ it is a new creation. But that means that it is the Act of One who, being Himself holy and having His end always in Himself, makes the whole end the very nature of His world's beginning, and sets its whole destiny working at the root of its origin. The new and final Humanity lies in the Act of its holy Redeemer; which Act is our light, clue, and cause through all the steps of the process through which it comes to be. That Act is an absolutely new beginning of the race, a second creation. And all the horrors of history in the first creation and its wars are parallel to the chaos (itself not without God) from which the first creation rose. But, since the new creation is much greater than the first, so the ferment caused in the social chaos by its gestation is greater and more terrible than anything we find on the level of the first. War is a far more dreadful thing than any ravage in the lower stages of nature. The collision of the Holy with the wickedness of man is more grave than the conflict of the Almighty with crude matter, or even crude mind. Redemption is a far more tragic thing than evolution and its struggles. The new creation must, of course, arise out of the first, for, though it is an absolute Act, it does not take place in an absolute way. But it is a more grave matter to regenerate the first creation into the second than it was to organise chaos into the first. The opposition of chaos, void and formless, was passive, but the opposition of the creature is active. It is a family quarrel, and they are the worst. It is not matter against force but will against will. It has behind it all the power of the freedom which makes the first creation what it chiefly is. So that it is really more true ethically to speak of God's goal as a New Humanity than as two stages oı states of the old Humanity—so long as we do not put the old and the new out of all organic connection whatever. It is no mere process that turns a child of nature into a son of man; far less is it such that turns a son of man into a Man of God. The Redeemer was not the mere agent of a process. He was the New Creator. He gave the race not only an impetus but a destiny. He is its destiny. It must stand at His judgment-seat. His salvation is its final teleology, its deep entelechy. And it is, in the atoning manner of it, the one theodicy, the vindication of God's justice in the process as well as of His glory in the goal.

CHAPTER IV

WHAT IS REDEMPTION?

In one more chapter I venture to continue the answer to that question, and now from the more religious side.

Nothing offers a future for such a world as this but its redemption. But by redemption what do we mean? We mean that the last things shall crown the first things, and that the end will justify the means, and the goal glorify a Holy God. We mean (if we allow ourselves theological language) an eschatology and a theodicy in it—a divine Heaven, a divine Salvation, and a divine Vindication in the result of history. But more. We mean a consummation which can only come by way of rescue and not mere growth. We mean rescue from evil by a God whose manner of it is moral, which is the act of a moral absolute, the act of a holy God doing justice to righteousness at any cost to Himself. We mean rectification of the present state of things on His own principles; that is, not mere rectification, mere straightening of a tangle, but justification on a transcendent plane of righteousness, the moral adjustment of man and God in one holy, loving, mighty, final, and eternal act. We certainly mean something more crucial than Meliorism.

Religion tends more and more, as we realise the state of things both by a larger knowledge and a finer sympathy, to centre on this matter of redemption. But how shall it be construed? Even philosophy now becomes redemptive—thanks largely to the deepening, the pointing, and the humanising of the Hegelian reconciliation by the pessimists. Philosophy cannot avoid considering the last things, and framing a doctrine of them. It answers their problem by its doctrine of the absolute, which corresponds to the theological doctrine of the holy. Both philosophy and theology agree on the existence of this ultimate power, and its exercise, either as mere pressure or as moral action, in subduing the atomic, chaotic, and discordant state of things. The question is, will it succeed ? Both religion and thought agree in the main that it will. But pessimism stands out. Serious and thorough pessimism alone dissents, holding that war is normal existence (if that be not a contradiction in terms, since war destroys all norms) and strife is fundamental to all things. This we may leave aside for the present, only noting how well Germany has learned from such teachers. We may agree that the absolute and holy will rule and round all, and we may go on to take note of the two very different forms this faith takes.

They turn on different views of the nature of this ever active and decisive power. For one it is immanent and pantheistic, for the other transcendental and personal. For the one tendency it means the presence and emergence in all things of the timeless and absolute *Being*, for the other the invasive action in all things of an influence akin less to thought than to will in *creating* and freedom in *becoming*. For the one the absolute and almighty inheres in the endless play of relative and fleeting things, and it forms their unity ; they cohere in it ; so that religion is the sense of the totality of all these relations breaking into light or flame. The absolute has such incandescent points, in which the finite knows that it is subdued and lost in the infinite. But an experience of this kind is not elevation to a new state of life and line of action : it is the suffusion of the soul, amid its natural chaos of impulse and mood, by a sense (first quick, then drowsy) of unity, harmony, and calm in the *grand être*. For the other view, however, the sense of the absolute or holy comes by the way of will and freedom rather than of imaginative thought. It brings less calm than confidence. It comes by the action of a freedom which can only exist as detached from the universal bond and released from the mere process of things, nay, as rounding and reacting upon them. The soul has to face the moral problem of growing surrender to the holy by effort, concentration, and obedience towards the selecting and creating Source. The great power is felt as moving in real action and not a stream of process. It lifts us, it does not merely bear us along. It gives us the very power to face, and even challenge it. It would have us stand up to it before we bow down. It lifts us at last to a living and humble union with itself, by the exercise of will and freedom on both sides. So that, while in the one system we have a new view of existence and its movement, new interpretation, in the other we have new life power, a new and living state of the soul, new vitality; and we have it by a free act of ours which places us, heart and conscience, in personal, living and congenial unity with the Holy in His Act. The one view thinks of a totality existing as a universe, the other of a holiness acting as creative, and of an evolution which works creatively, *i.e.* by way of a contributing freedom instead of an overriding process. One tends to pantheistic mysticism, with the whole at each point, the other to faith in a personalist creation, with its goal at the close—except in so far as it is always in the Creator whom we meet at each point.

Observe that it is a redemption either way. In the one case it is a redemption from the atom to the all, from the fractional to the whole, from the fleeting to the firm, from the unreal to the real. In the other case it is a release from law to liberty, from self to sacrifice, from the imperfect to the perfect, from the crude to the complete, from strife not to peace only but to victory, from sin to righteousness. On the one line we tend to pantheism for a philosophy, and to Buddhism for a religion; on the other we move to voluntaryism, Judaism, and Christianity.

Now it is quite true that neither of these is without some influence on the other, and useful influence. But in the long run a choice must be made. And it is not a speculative choice but a practical. That is to say, it involves the disposal of ourselves, and not simply the selection of a theory. It is moral and religious. We have to ask which of the two forms of redemption really deserves the name, which sets us really free, which makes more for religious energy and moral effect. Is it that there is one line on which we lose the soul, and one on which we find it? Does one make more than the other for the holy, and give it freer course with us? Few can doubt that in this respect the difference is vast; nor will most people doubt that for moral life we must choose the second. To go to what is most painfully and crucially under our eyes—Germany as a whole has chosen the former, and it has cost her her soul, her moral soul. As a people she knows everything of culture and nothing of salvation, of redemption nothing. She has come to worship wholes instead of respecting souls; and the whole she worships is not Humanity but an egoist whole, and especially in the form of the State. As a consequence she has thrown overboard public morality in the name and idolatry of sheer power. The State is the moral authority. She has expressly claimed for the powerful State the right to decide when moral control ends and succumbs to egoist interests. That is, the nation relapses to the worship of Wotan and the cult of Loki, and confesses its real God to be nature force and process, the ancient prince of hell in mail of craft and power. And this has brought her to the passion of world empire, merciless skill, and war upon Humanity. She has lost the sense and the value of the individual, both his liberty and his responsibility. She has overridden conscience by the State, and left it for dead. The people are pawns in the war-game.

The man is merged in the soldier. And his warfare is with the Kingdom of God—whereof the Allies are *ad hoc* the undeserving pillars.

So, if we care supremely for the moral soul and the Kingdom of God, it is the second of these two forms of redemption we must take. It is the more personal view, which lays the stress on choice rather than thought, on crisis rather than order, on free will rather than fated force, on constant creation rather than perpetual process, on a first free creation which commits us, for our perfecting, to a second freer still.

But even apart from moral results, the pantheistic doctrine has but a spurious appearance of unity, if we criticise it on philosophic grounds alone. Its apparent unity is an importation: it is not a discovery. We bring it with us, we do not find it there. What we find is a mass of relations. And what seems more is really something we carry to that mass, and read into it. We make an illicit, though unconscious, contribution of the unity of our own personality, the unifying order of thought inseparable from personality. We transfer the sense of our own unity and reality to the world, and thus we hypostatise the category of relationship in the mass of things, instead of discovering an absolute which transcends and holds it.

But, if there is to be any importation, let us be thorough. If we ourselves are items of an inter-related universe, the unifying contribution must be to us rather than by us. Let us go through with this matter of contribution, and rise to the thought of creation. The contribution *to us* is everything. It is existence, and all that enriches existence. It is creation. The one contributor to the universe, the Creditor that buys out all the rest is its Creator. This makes a moral relation possible, first, between the world and its source, its absolute, and, second, between its items. This makes freedom, and makes for freedom. It gives us that power, and it develops the gift. This is the great mysticism—that of conscience blent with conscience. Being with being might mingle, but will with will!—what will overcome hate? The weakness of the mysticism which is more imaginative than moral, and more inward than historic, is that it tends away from the idea of creation to 'eternal process moving on,' and to the absorption of our freedom and responsibility in that infinite stream. It does not create, therefore it does not really renew. It only swells. It does not add the new thing, which will or freedom alone does. It only puts things in a certain fresh or seemly light, without warm power. Mere process cannot be self-fed. Suns burn out. It does not save: it only develops a vaster and more complex mass, waiting and groaning to be saved. It presents an idea of unity which has nothing in it to withstand the constant drop in temperature to a freezing equality everywhere. It is light without power—an auroral light and not a solar. It may quell troublesome desire, and police spontaneity (*more teutonico*), but it does not bring new life. But the relativism, the imperfection, the anomalies, the tragedies can only be lost in an Absolute which is real to life, passion, and personality; they can only be made good in a moral Absolute, in the active revelation of the Holy One, and the Apocalypse of the Son of God. We must arrive, either by our faith, or our thought, or by both, at an Absolute very different from a mere sum of relations hypostatised. We must have one with initiative, one creative, a living and holy Will; which, having made the soul, alone knows the secret of the lock, and can enter it, and sit down with it, and sup, and rear it to a new creature through communion bestowed or restored. The communion itself rises, in a sublimation, to an ever closer union of will and will, and so to perfection. And this applies not to single souls only but, by the same divine principle and Act, to the soul and life of Humanity. But, for man's historic and evil life, for the life of the race, this means redemption by something else than a diffused process—by a concentrated Act, with an eternal and universal bearing. For an act must be at a centre, even if it be qualitatively an infinite centre, as man is in the universe. Activity only diffused or processional is but movement, it is not action; it is not of will, it has no centre and no moral value. The redemption, therefore, of a race with a conscience and a history means a historic Act of redemption on the part of the Holy, controlling the whole of the race's career, and in command of all the cataclysms and tragedies that seem at times to eclipse its sun. His loving-kindness breaks through every midnight of the soul. And this Act assures the perfecting, both of the race and of its units and of each through the other, in a reciprocity founded in that of Creator and creature, Redeemer and saint—perhaps even Father and Son. It means the glory, honour, and immortality of the one in the other, by an Act whose nature is moral to the pitch of a holiness that destroys all sin and guilt by the omnipotence of righteousness.

This great, and righteous, and blessed goal then—what is it? We speak of the end of the world. But (it has been said) in any great sense of the word world, it can have no end. Our deeper views of creation, and of the relation of the creature to the Creator, do not allow us to think of the universe as an external and mechanical product of His, which He could destroy and make another. The existence of the universe is too closely bound up with the being of God for that. Its life is the immanence of the Transcendent. It does not emerge into Eternity, which is not simply a beyond. The infinite is the content of a finite which holds of the Eternal. The world belongs to God in a deeper sense than being His property. The body is not but the property of the soul. The world holds of God. It cannot therefore have an end, as it had no beginning, in the popular sense of the words; it has a consummation. The universe is not a mere phase of the Infinite which passes like a vapour. It is not a mere parenthesis otiose to an eternal context. It is not a mere scaffolding, not a mere collapsible tent. We cannot strictly speak of the end of the world; we can only speak of the end of certain worlds within the world. Stardust is still a constituent of the world. Extinct suns still have a place in systems. And extinct systems may mean a re-adjustment of the balance of power in space, but they need not mean the winding-up of the universe.

When we do speak of the end of the world, we really mean the end of man. And, if there be a redemption at all, that end is neither in dust nor fire. The end of Humanity can but mean the return of man to God, in free worship, humble service, and intelligent communion. It means the consummation of the souls that began as His natural creatures and end as redeemed sons. For spiritual personality is a growth through the creative discipline of life, and especially through its tragedies. The supreme tragedy becomes, in the Cross of Christ, the vehicle of the eternal Redemption, and the Source of the New Creation. Man's end is not dissolution but Eternity, an active communion in the Life divine. A communion it is, and no mere immersion. It is not mere fusion in the Divine, which, for a being like man, would be extinction. And no mere endless existence could be a true end for man. It could be no consummation. Immortality is much more than just going on. Were it not more it would be the burden of Tithonus. Eternity is not duration. The true end is the completion of that schooling of soul, will, and person which earthly life divinely means, and which for God's side is constant new creation and its joy. It is perfect and active union with God's active Will, the barter of its love, and its secure intercommunion. It is the surrender to God, not of our personality, not of our existence as persons, but of our person, of our egoism as persons; for the living God is God of the living not of the dead. It is a kingdom of souls as ends that realise themselves, though only in the gift of the Spirit, which descends upon us rather than mounts through us. We face here a great paradox. By grace it is *given* souls to have life *in themselves.* The great end, therefore, is not even an immortality sentimentalised—a metaphysical, rational, and credible immortality sentimentalised; but it is a moral realm of persons made perfect on a universal and eternal scale by the gift of a holy God. It is the self-realisation of the Holy. It is the Divine *Commedia* on the scale of all existence. To the whole of Humanity, with faith and hope eclipsed by world catastrophe, the infinite and most merciful Majesty yet says, 'Fear not, little flock, it is the Father's good pleasure to *give* you the Kingdom.' And, '*Si quis amavit novit quid haec vox clamat.*'

The chief cause of our being unhinged by catastrophe is twofold. First, that we have drawn our faith from the order of the world instead of its crisis, from the integrity of the moral order rather than from the tragedy of its recovery in the Cross. And, even if we start there, the second error is that we have been more engrossed with the ill we are saved from than with Him who saves us, and the Kingdom for which we are saved. We are more taken up with the wrongs so many men have to bear than with the wrong God has to bear from us all—God who yet atones and redeems in giving us a Kingdom which is always His in reality and ours in reversion. It is not as if God first redeemed, and, having thus prepared the ground, brought in the Kingdom; but He redeemed us by bringing in the Kingdom, and setting it up in eternal righteousness and Eternal Life. The Cross of Christ is not the preliminary of the Kingdom; it is the Kingdom breaking in. It is not the clearing of the site for the heavenly city; it is the city itself descending out of heaven from God.

CHAPTER V

SALVATION THEOLOGICAL BUT NOT SYSTEMATIC

A MORAL salvation, the final and foregone conquest of guilt by judging Grace and searching Love, is our only warrant *in extremis* for believing in the radical order and final purpose of the world. But such a salvation presents not only the ground but also the contours of that belief. It is a *fides formata*. It is more than very sanguine. For I have already suggested that a theodicy must rest on a theology, and an evangelical theology; and this must be emphasised. Being Christians we believe in the world as saved, and not merely as settled, and in human nature as redeemed and not as excellent, as regenerated and not merely as educated. We believe that all is well, even if all goes not well. What we are perfectly sure about is something fundamental and eternal—God's saving relation to man, and man's saved relation to God. It is a saved relation, it is not merely a filial; nor are we but fostered into Eternal Life. The greater our need, the greater His deed; Lazarus dead brought Him as He never came before. Our worst need casts us entirely outside our own resources. All is well with the world, since its Saviour has it finally and fully in hand. Victory awaits us because the victory is won. Our victory is the world's destiny, because it is already God's gift. I feel, of course, that these statements rest on a theological groundwork for which there is here no space. We are more than conquerors through Him that loved us;

we are redeemed. We are beloved into a destiny we never achieved, and could never love ourselves into. The root of the moral matter, when we rise to this region where all earth's ethic and history draw to a solemn head, is not that we love, but that we are beloved—beloved by the Holy, beloved, therefore, into righteousness. It is not that we love, but that we trust such righteous Love, not that we sacrifice, but that we trust the Cross. All our divine knowledge springs from being known, and being loved even better even than we are known. Herein is Love—not that we loved, but that He did. If He did not, if we cannot be sure He did, we can have no teleology of the world. No human hate can thwart God's Kingdom so long as His holy Love holds ; which cannot fail, for it is His Omnipotence. Only He must be allowed His own way of showing it, and giving it effect. About the strategy of that He mostly keeps His own counsel. Love He has given us, and faith, with Himself to love, trust, and obey. What He has not given us is a scheme of rational optimism, or a visible process of good, dawning and spreading to its perfect day. He has given us no programme of happy things. The totality of the world, its wholeness and unity in Him, consists not in its being a system, but in its having a meaning, and in meaning Him. Yet these designs which we do not find are the things we expect when we start from the hopes of nature instead of the faith of Grace. The Church itself is ruled by this pagan dream. It offers a God consecrating nature's initial instinct with His benediction, as a marriage service might ; and then it stands by with the Cross to console or stay us when the scheme fails and the hopes come to grief. But that is not the method of God's Revelation in the Cross. It does not come in to grout the gaps in nature, not simply to bless nature, but to change it, to make a new earth from a foundation in a new heaven—from a new exercise of God's divinest power, that of creating. We are apt to look—our cultured

Christianity especially looks—for a world of symmetry rather than a world of reconciliation, for a world complete in a harmony of parts instead of perfect in a reconciliation of persons. We even think the Christian aspiration is to aim at harmony with the character of Jesus instead of reconciliation through Him with the holiness of God. Sometimes, if we try to enter such reconciliation, it is with the feeling, more or less latent, that it is a preliminary or a surrogate. We think that it is a means or a proxy for something which will be really more satisfactory, but which is deferred, namely, the vision of a universe thoroughly co-ordinated and lubricated, with a place found at last for the pieces of the puzzle which were quite refractory before. That we think would be heaven—the whole business of goodness completely organised. We lay more stress on structure, machinery, swing, and amenity than on purpose, worth, and costly righteousness, in our world of things. We want to see all things palpably working together for good. But this would be sight and not faith. Is it not a relic of the notional religion which has been the Church's bane, a survival of the scientific passion to understand things instead of the moral passion to commune with persons? Our ideal world is thought to contain a scheme of truth rather than a burthen of meaning. Even the Kingdom of God is viewed as a grand social fabric working in the harmony of love, instead of the divine Kingship, a grand common relation of souls—of God to us, and of us to God—from which a heavenly order flows *sans dire.*

We see not yet all things, but we see Jesus. There is a limitation in the teleology of salvation which is really a concentration. What we are given is not an orderly survey of the area of salvation, with all its lines streaming to a head of fruition; but it is a vast certainty of its reality, its principle, and its victory. We have not a plan of operations but a goal of values; not the strategy of Providence, but the finality of Redemption. God's revelation does not range the field of history, it goes to its centre—to its moral centre, to the site both of its power and its impotence, to the conscience. The matter is not one of speculative nor of scientific theology. It is ethical. The certainty is morally mystic. The conscience is the creative region of all history, and when that is set right with its holy Creator all will be right in tail. It is there that Humanity is one —in that which God has done for the conscience of the race, in the Reconciliation which undoes guilt, and makes moral peace and endless power for the soul and for the race. Man is most surely one only in his divine destiny, only as redeemed. Our Christian faith is that we are redeemed, that the end of our soul is sure, since Christ has become responsible for it. But He took charge of it by no private arrangement with units, but in an Act of Salvation which new created the whole world. Therefore in Him we are as sure that the Kingdom of God is the grand goal of the universe as we are of our own soul's destiny. What reconciles my warring conscience in Christ, and makes me one in my pacified soul, since it *is* in Christ, certifies to me also the destined unity of the race. And in this faith we know that the Kingdom not only awaits all things and affairs, but crucially subdues them and growingly pervades them as their informing principle. For our faith the victorious Christ is involved and dominant, He is immanent and transcendent, in the movement of the world. But not only so; He coincides with its consummation. For man to live is Christ. All things are (so to say) tied up in Christ and His Cross. Every stage of man's progress must go to His judgment-seat; and it is progress only as it may be so measured there. It is true progress only by its relation to Him, His Holiness, and His Eternity, and not by what we can see and assess as its contribution to progress as we deem it—even to what seems moral and spiritual progress. Progress, as an object and a standard, has played its part for the time being, and must wait in the wings. This shattering war shows that. The supreme object of creation and of history (I have said) is to bring every man before the judgment-seat of the grace of Christ. It is not to provide each with a minimum of three acres and a cow, and keep his pot boiling.

So our certain faith in a divine goal not only depends on our faith in redemption, but it is determined in its large form by God's way of redemption. And this is not evolutionary improvement and elevation shining more and more to the perfect day; but it is crisis, judgment, atonement, suffering, moral revolution, and re-creation from a new centre. The only possible belief in a teleology of the world (if it is to be thorough) is a religious solution of a moral issue. It is that evangelical faith in God's holy atonement which is the trust and burthen of the Church. The Gospel of the Church, of Grace to conscience, issuing from the greatest moral crisis of Time and of God, is the key of history. The destiny to salvation is the *primum movens*, the essential, formative, and dominant thing in the history of Humanity. The stream is often forced underground, but it never loses volume, power, or instinct for its goal. Its object is to produce a realm of personalities not only moral but holy, and not only holy but redeemed into a holiness they had lost the power ever to achieve.

It has often been charged upon historians of the Church, and justly, that they have marred that history by disregard of the world around it, by treating 'profane' history as that history itself might treat zoology. But the fault is not all on one side. An even greater mistake is made by those who treat the history of the world with no vital reference to the history of its finest product,—the Church, its moral principle, and its central message for man. It is only in the Church's Gospel, the Gospel of a Church in organic yet miraculous connection with the natural man, that we find a teleology of history. But, if the world's teleology is thus religiously sure, by the same religion it is determined as a moral teleology. And it is determined not simply by the weight of a moral order more ubiquitous and constant than we can experience, but by the moral crisis of the Cross whose finality we can experience, ending in a Kingdom to whose righteousness all things else are added. With the Kingdom of God civilisation is but thrown in ; it is a by-product of the Kingdom ; and its pace must be set by the Kingdom's ethic on peril of judgment and collapse. If civilisation collapsed, the Divine Kingdom is yet immune from its doom. 'The City of God remaineth.'

> 'I saw . . . O brother, 'mid far sands
> The palm-tree-cinctured city stands,
> Bright white beneath, as Heaven, bright blue,
> Leans o'er it, while the years pursue
> Their course, unable to abate
> Its Paradisal laugh at fate ! '

It is the nature and faith of this Kingdom—the faith and not simply the ideal of a Kingdom which is actually set up in the Cross—that makes Christianity universal. It is universal, not empirically, not yet actually, but potentially in its nature, genius, and destiny. It cannot but be missionary. We believe in the world because we believe in its goal, and we believe in its goal because we believe supremely in its God, and consult His Glory more even than the happiness of men. And we believe in God because of His Christ, His Cross, His victory, and His Gospel.

It is often thought remarkable that modern Protestant missions should have arisen out of a creed whose aspect was so *borné*, and whose sympathy was so limited, as Calvinism, and the second- or third-rate Calvinism of the eighteenth century. And, no doubt, to our humanist notions of religion this is a great paradox. But that is due to such notions—to our anthropocentric point of view. These missionary pioneers of a century ago began with the glory of God rather than the pity of man. Their attitude to men was sometimes unsympathetic—especially to their religions. But the lesson is that, in spite of such defects, a creed which starts from the glory of God has more power for man's welfare than one that is founded in the welfare of man alone. Calvin, with all the traits in him that are now easily and cheaply branded as inhuman, was the saviour of evangelical religion for the world as even Luther was not; and he has been worth more to modern democracy than his great humanist rival and complement Rousseau. If we study God's freedom as supremely as Calvin did, He will see to ours. A theocentric creed has more and longer blessing for man than an anthropocentric. It is the divine in our creed that makes it last, though it may be the humane that makes it attract. For it gives us certainty as to the last result. Our steps are not then tentative, but apostolic—dogmatic in the great and royal sense. It gives us the final teleology in the Kingdom as part of our certainty of the Gospel. Missions have languished to their present serious state with the growth in the last fifty years of humanitarian Christianity—which tends to exhaust our Christian beneficence on the things that come nearer us than Christ, on the needs, wrongs, and woes nearest us at home, and therefore most keenly felt. Our religion has come to live on sympathy rather than faith; and sympathy will not carry what religion has to bear or faith to do. The ground of missions is neither generous pity nor 'sailing orders' from Christ, but inspiration, the inspiration and genius of His world Gospel. It is the inspiration of His 'finished work,' and therefore the faith of His sure Kingdom as the last goal, the divine destiny, and the deepest *nisus* of the whole world.

I spoke a little ago of the bane of a notional religion and the reduction of the theology at the heart of Christian faith to a scheme of truths. I alluded to the treatment of Revelation as something propositional rather than redemptive, and even of the Kingdom of God as the organisation of society by love between its members instead of by their common and holy relation to a loving God. I spoke of the way the true idea of Revelation was destroyed by being viewed as the conveyance of truth about God and His action, instead of God's actual coming and acting; so that the religion which responds to it dropped to a mode of creed, an orthodoxy, instead of rising to personal faith in the Saviour. I have dwelt also on the Object of our faith as One acting more than teaching, One to be trusted and not traced. I said that religion was power more than truth, and warmth more than light alone. I said that even an essentially moral process like regeneration had come, through the severance from ethical processes like atonement and justification, to need to be moralised—to be re-claimed from its baptismal or its emotional impotence, and treated as a re-creation really conscious, personal, and holy, and therefore moral in its nature and genius. I should like here to take up these points, and dwell on them further, because the passion for founding on a rational justification of God, whether in a historic strategy of Providence or a scientific scheme of belief, is one that leaves our faith in a divine teleology helpless in great crises. It is staggered, if not killed, when historic progress seems to end around us in a social collapse and a moral anarchy in which everything is held lawful to a powerful state. But if the moral soul is anchored on the Gospel of the Cross and Kingdom of God in a historic crisis really greater than any war, it cannot be swept away by any currents or storms in history. We are more than conquerors through Him that loved us and gave Himself for us. This means not only that we are conquerors and more, but that, even did we not feel conquerors, we should be more than victorious by our share in the final victory in which Love overcame the world.

But, if faith be stayed only on the observed growth of moral and spiritual progress, if it be but optimist, if it turn on the evidences of amelioration, the growth in humanity, and the progress of nations, it is at the mercy of such shocks as the present, in which progress commits suicide, and which bring to the ground in a great fall the creeds built on the shifting dunes.

The reaction against theological system has run high in the Free Churches, where it has gone so far as to make people widely indifferent to all theological interior for faith. The Love of God, for instance, has been removed from its New Testament setting. It has been treated as the mere superlative of romantic love. It has been detached from the idea of propitiation with which the Apostles identify it (1 John iv. 10), and regarded as an infinite dilation of human affection (where the real revelation is held to be). Judgment is viewed but as a device of the Father instead of a constituent of His Fatherhood as holy. Little wonder then that love has gone thin in the expansion, and lost power. It has ceased in the process to be understood as Holy Love. (I speak but generally and broadly, not of universal features, but of dangerous tendencies.) It has been de-ethicised in the sense that it has its ethic but as a sequel and supplement, and not as its intrinsic principle. Its holiness has been held to have no reaction in judgment, and to need no such assertion in the Cross which founds our faith, but only appreciation as faith went on. The atonement of the Holy to the Holy has fallen to be a mere theologoumenon, instead of standing as the moral focus and crisis of God's conscience and man's in history actual and practical. Accordingly, the moral action of love has been reduced to social conduct, its holy quality to passion intense in quantity, and its passion to sentiment. This generates an atmosphere, either stuffy or airy, in which the last and greatest issues between God and man cannot breathe. Thought is trivialised into interests neither universal nor fundamental, neither tragic nor glorious, but just drab or humdrum ; so that adequate treatment of ultimate things is dismissed by the sentimentalists as obscurity. The ministry of Eternal Grace sinks into the ministries of passing help ('This ought ye to have done without leaving the other undone'). Churches are frayed into ribbons of small but kindly endeavour. Sacraments are deserted for socialities (as in the Corinthian Church). And there issues from them no moral Word piercing and commanding enough to reach the public soul at the depths to which it is stirred by a catastrophe of the first rank. The name of Jesus is dear, but Christ is no Leader and Commander to the people.

If we turn our eye upon the other great section of the Church, on Anglicanism, we find a somewhat different situation. Instead of rational morality and sentimental impression, we find mystic (not to say magic) sacramentalism and creedalism, crossing, and often crushing, the moral timbre of the evangelical note which makes a Church a Church. We find what may be compendiously called the reign of Chalcedonism, the preference of theosophy to theology, of God's thought to His action ; the creedal, institutional, official note, the action of the schematic, non-ethical, non-prophetic, canonical spirit in construing Revelation and Providence. We find it even where there may be considerable criticism of the formal Chalcedonian theology, and much effort to simplify belief to the measure of the current mind. One effect of this theosophic and institutional habit of mind is that the Anglican scholar, when he tries to modernise a doctrine like the Incarnation, tends to prefer a subliminal basis to one theological, ethical, and evangelical. By Chalcedonism is meant the standardised type of religion represented ecclesiastically in Catholicism, theologically in what is called the Athanasian Creed. As to that creed exception is here taken less to its matter than to its manner. So far as the matter goes, if the doctrine of the Trinity (which certainly is at the heart of Christianity) was to be expressed in the intellectual conditions of the fourth century it probably could not have been better done. I do not even object sweepingly to the damnatory note. There are not nearly enough preachers who preach, nor people who take home, the reality of damnation, or the connection of liberty with it. The vice in the creed is the association of salvation or damnation with forms which, though they are not intellectualist, are yet much too intellectual and too little ethical for general faith, and must be taken on external authority. There must, indeed, be external authority, but not on the thing that makes a soul Christian and settles its Eternity. The creed, I have said, is not intellectualist. The reality and power of Redemption work behind it all, and really make its ruling interest. But it is couched in elaborate terms drawn admirably from the metaphysic of the day, but reflecting the undue primacy of that metaphysic. It labours with a machinery which has long ceased to be equal to the needs and habits of the Christian conscience. It consecrates unduly the patristic stage of the Church, at the cost of the New Testament norm. Its genius is too alien to the New Testament note, and the one charter of the Church there—to the ethical and experimental quality of the Gospel. It is too dominantly philosophical, and too little moral, to correspond with the New Testament Gospel, and to its new creative power. Its conception of Eternal Life is not the New Testament one, being the physical purified by the quasi-physical, rather than the natural overcome by the spiritual. Redemption, I say, is indeed the great note of the creed ; but it has begun, nay, it has gone some way, to be unmoralised. Attention is deflected from the New Covenant, which was Christ's first concern, to the new nature, which He does not speak of. Interest is removed even from the new man to the new nature. It is removed from the Christian adjustment of the holy conscience of God and the guilty conscience of Man in the Cross; and it is turned upon certain metaphysical implicates, which were imported more than inspired into faith, which were accepted rather than produced by it, and which can be very interesting to the morally unregenerate mind. I will not say that these were intruded into faith, because there is a place for them there; but at best they are its scientific postulates rather than its religious objects or products. The result of the importance given to this element in the Chalcedonian mentality (so strangely dull still to the Evangelical note) is this, that for the conditions of salvation the lay Christian, who does not understand a scientific theology detached from experience, must depend on the word and authority of the Church which does. His mere assent gives him his Christian status. From which implicit assent he *descends* to such personal experience as may thereupon be open to him. That is a false foundation and an inverted movement. It is a *ὕστερον πρότερον*. It puts creed before salvation, as if revelation were theology instead of theological, as if it were truth instead of redemption, a theme rather than a power. The moral method, when the Gospel is presented with the prestige of the Church, is to rise from experience to assent, from experience of the Gospel to assent to the Church theology of it, from life doctrines we can directly verify to thought doctrines we cannot, from experience of Redemption to assent to Incarnation, from personal religion to corporate dogmatic. But to begin with either the doctrine of the Trinity or the Incarnation, and descend to an atoning Redemption (as Catholicism did, both in its history and its principle) is to take the note of the Gospel out of the Church, and to depreciate a Christianity of personal experience for one of formal status, in which the man is ranged rather than changed. It throws the accent of the national religion off the conscience, off the moral nature and action of the sacred Word. It means beginning with something which we do not understand, but which we take because it is taught by Bible or Church, and then going on to make this acceptance the condition of benefiting in experience. The Incarnation, for the lay mind, means the miraculous birth, which, as you cannot verify it in experience, must be taken on the authority of the Bible or the Church. For others it means either a metaphysical truth taken on the same authority ; or it is a moral reality rising (as in the New Testament) from the experience of forgiveness in the Gospel and from the certainty that Christ has there done on us a work that none but God could do. Its metaphysic is a metaphysic either of substantial being or of moral action on the divine scale. Is the former not the Catholic note on the whole—Roman or Anglican ? Is it not in tune with the sacramentarian idea, with its stress on the conversion of a substance rather than a soul ? Is it not more Catholic than Evangelical, more metaphysical than moral, descending in use to be more magical than either ? The central doctrine, it is said, is the Incarnation, which gives value to all human relations, theological truth, or sacraments. It means a process, largely unthinkable, whereby the infinite nature of God and the finite nature of man received an adjustment capable of embodiment in historic conditions—something no more verifiable in experience than the miraculous birth. It is to be taken therefore on the authority of a Church of experts settling it in councils whose effective number and competency are a matter of varying opinion. Begin with believing that,[1] then you have a divine ground for ethic and a divine foundation for conscience ; then also you will meet the prior condition for profiting by the divine Atonement of your guilt. The Incarnation (it is said) affects your whole nature, but the Atonement only the moral part of it, where guilt lies.

[1] I speak but of the theological method, not the religious experience of the Church with this theology.

(Think of conscience being treated but as a part of man! No wonder Christendom suffers from a double morality.) The Semi-Pelagian note is then easily regarded as the true one, and guilt is not held to be entire impotence with God. Begin everything with Christ's relation to human nature and not to human will or conscience. Begin by believing in an Incarnation more or less philosophical on the authority either of the Church or of the Bible. Begin by postulating, in a Coleridgean way, that humanity was 'constituted' in Christ, then the Atonement can receive its sequential place in the system, and Redemption play its due part in your faith. That is, begin with metaphysic more or less diluted, or you will not arrive at religion. Begin with a faith in such an Incarnation, else you can have no saving faith in Redemption. Is this not a ὕστερον πρότερον? Is it not putting religion on another than a moral foundation, and giving it another than a moral quality for life? Doubtless for thought, for theological science, Incarnation is the logical *prius*. It is at the rational base of Atonement, of Redemption, which was God's offering up of Himself in Christ. But that is to say it was God's Act in Christ more than His mere presence. The metaphysic is one of ethic, of action, not of being; it is of will rather than thought. The Church's message is not there first for the thinkers, but for the active world—for the world of conscience, for the theology of experience. The Church indeed must be theological —if it would but go about its theology in the experient rather than the expert way. And for experience it is the atoning Redemption that is at the practical base of belief in the Incarnation and prescribes its nature. And, if we invert that order, as the school theology did, is it not bound to affect the whole relation of religion to ethic and to society. Is it not likely to postpone the moral genius of Christianity; to articulate the Cross into the moral order of nature instead of finding it to be the crisis and judgment of nature and the natural conscience; to consecrate the *lex naturae* rather than convert it; to canonise the decent and conventional elder brother rather than the prodigal forgiven much; and to make any ethical demand which seems to revolutionise the natural ethic, or invert its values, seem extravagance? The Chalcedonian type of belief, on Catholic or Protestant ground, does not appeal to man's conscience and then rise to his intelligence. It begins with his intelligence, and may or may not go on to conscience. It does not convert a man, and then make a theologian of him; it makes a theologian of him, and then as to conversion—well, if it do not come, there was the baptismal regeneration whereby to escape the worst if we neglect so great a moral salvation. In Anglican writings (of the most valuable kind otherwise) it is startling to find how the element of ethic and of atonement in the nature of Christ has been submerged by the sacramental and moral insight reduced to moral interest.

But I am not here dwelling on the unmoralising effect of Chalcedonian sacramentarianism, but rather of what may be called its propositionalism. They both act in the non-ethical direction; but, as I am discussing a religion of schematic teleology and theodicy, it is less the magical than the logical perversion of Christian faith that lies in my track. Chalcedonism is orthodox rationalism. And I am complaining that this intellectualising of faith has unmoralised, and often demoralised, it. Both the Church and the world have been led to look for God's self-justification in a schematic or strategic way instead of a moral, in a system of coherent truth or in an order of things palpably telic and beneficent, instead of a Person's Act of crisis, judgment, and conquest. They have sought it by sight not faith. We have been set to trace God's thought or process instead of trusting His absolute Grace in Christ; and we have sought its moral victory less in a kingdom of divine relation than in forms of social organisation. In this way thought has unmoralised faith, and, by turning it into sight, begun the slope to its demoralisation. It has not found the prime object of faith in the eternal moral Act of God in history—an Act central and fontal, new-creative and revolutionary for the conscience ; but it has made that object (if an act at all) to be an act largely metaphysical, like the Incarnation, the faith of which would provide the only effective access to the moral Act of Atonement. In a word, faith has become academised, then macadamised and trodden underfoot. Its gigantic frame is tied down with packthreads innumerable and effective.

We are apt to confine our criticism of the systematic passion to theology or Church. We do not stop to reflect that the objection taken to these really is that, as systems, they collide with another system which is our own hobby. Only we call it a practical system, efficiency or results. Such like names we use for our ideal scheme which the other schemes seem to retard. We construct a plan, programme, polity, or Utopia ; and things go well as they make for it, ill as they do not. We call its fulfilment success. We plant our ambition for it on God. We set our heart on it as a piece of our religion. We regard its success as a proof of its truth and right. We really care for the success more than for either the right or truth. We believe in these just as they work. With their failure in the machinery of things faith goes. A certain practical construction of things gets the allegiance due to Revelation. A visible teleology takes the place of a sure faith. The success measures the cause. Old Hebraism and new Pragmatism meet. Goodness ought to work. Failure is our moral impeachment. If the thing do not go it should not go. Adversity but registers hidden guilt. If we win, does it follow we were right ? If we lose, is it because we were wrong ? The failure of the Son of God was the victory that overcame the whole world. Yet we have even preachers telling the public, with an incredible stupidity, that to prove Christianity to yourself you must try it, and find how well it goes. As a matter of fact, you cannot try it till you believe it. And you have not got it till you are thinking more of your God than of your success, and trusting Him most when your success fails—as Christ did on the Cross which was God's real success with the world. We worship success, we do not believe in the omnipotence of the holy revealed in service.

It is no wonder that in the circumstances Christian ethic should become a more or less otiose appendix to natural, nor that Christian faith should become too dependent on natural continuity, natural evolution, or the meeting of natural expectation. It is not strange that in these circumstances New Testament morality should become a sectional, or even sectarian, affair compared with a Nicomachean ethic or a Hellenic catholicity. Chalcedonism is a Christianity based on culture, not to say ruled by it; and Germany, both by its Byzantinism and its militarism, has shown where that ends. It ends in a national character in whose formation the barrack has had much more to do than the Church, and the New Testament hardly anything at all. How far is our own national character due to similar egoist influences, and especially to the same neglect of Christian nurture? We still await a culture based on Christianity, *i.e.* less on Christ's teaching than on the moral regeneration flowing from God's moral Act and crisis of the Cross, creative and supreme for the whole race, and rich with all the fullness of Christ. It is through this Act alone that we rise to the faith, fullness, and power of the Incarnation[1] that is within it. It is His Atonement in its experience value, it is the rich and regenerative oblation of the race's conscience there, it is the Eternal Life created in us as moral beings there, that give us access to the real meaning of His Incarnation and found the true, the evangelical, Catholicism. It is such faith that finds meaning in the Incarnation as a moral Act, beyond mere

[1] Experience is the method but not the measure of faith.

prodigy, meaning for the moral soul that makes us men—even if guilty men. However we speculate, we know nothing of any Incarnation except what our conscience finds in the atoning Redemption and its implicates of Reconciliation. A holy God self-atoned in Christ is the moral centre of the sinful world. Our justification by God has its key in God's justification of Himself. If we begin with culture we shall end with crises; but if we begin with crisis at the Cross all culture is added to it.

Chalcedonism, therefore, construed as the primacy of the formal, systematic, and institutional, puts a premium upon a non-ethical type of religion. It breeds in society a Catholicity more correct than creative, more soothing than searching: it creates a conscience which is the victim of order rather than the beneficiary of grace, and which therefore is the victim of despair when the order collapses, because it was not in crisis that its trust was born. This is the antithesis of the true evangelical note; whose disengagement from it began, but only began, in the Reformation; and which has been prolonged most vitally on the more Calvinistic side, the more historic and progressive side, of the Reformation. The present cataclysm should make an end of Lutheranism, or reduce it to the Teutonic sect. Chalcedonism means the substitution for experience of truth, and metaphysical truth, on the external authority of a Church over the intelligence. It means the substitution of this in a baptismal regeneration for a moral experience (forgiveness, regeneration, and reconciliation), on the liberating authority to the conscience of the Gospel Word. It is this propositional surrogate for the moral experience of regeneration which has such a de-ethicising effect on the Catholic side, as sentimental impressionism saps moral divination on the other.[1]

[1] To be just, I should like to say here that such a view of the Incarnation as Westcott represents does not fall under my criticism of Chalcedonism. It is much too ethical in its nature; and Mr. Mozley points out to me how

It is a position too incongruous to be permanent, that Churches which are one upon their fundamental theology should be out of communion with each other upon its institutional aspect (as is the case with Anglicanism and the other Churches of the country); or that, being one in every other respect, they should be institutionally divided, and even rival, on a rite, as is the case between the Baptists and all other Churches. It is erecting into a primary place something which in the genius of Christianity is but secondary. It is making the canonical first and the evangelical second, and dividing the Gospel by that which is not gospel, but only exists for its sake. It seems a singular thing, and it must surely become intolerable, that, in the face of a world so dreadful that it takes all the strength of Christianity to believe in the reign of God in it or His redemption of it, believers who pray apart to the same God, the same Christ, the same atoning Saviour, should refuse to join in public prayer because of institutional differences, and the freezing there of what was meant to be pliant to occasion. It seems to point to some deep and damaging dislocation of the canonical, institutional, patristic, medieval element (the yet precious element) of tradition. It indicates some undue and unconscious influence on the religious education of many minds by this aspect of things, so much more academic than ethical, more traditional than evangelical, so inadequate to a day of judgment like the present, which breaks open a new time and a new world.

I would repeat that the criticism on which I have ventured, both of the Anglican Church and the rest, has been but very general, and it has referred to what I should de-

it has at least concurred with a new era of social interests within Anglicanism. But even this less metaphysical and more religious view is less thorough morally than is required by the nature of the Gospel before it began to speak the language of the Logos, and while it took in earnest the idea of a new creation and a *regeneration of the conscience.*

scribe as tendencies rather than features. For, if one is to be just and candid, there is on both sides the ethical note both of moral creation and discipline, which is *the* note and blessing of Puritanism, which Puritanism selected and pressed for continuation from the Catholic tradition. It would be hard to say whether there was now more of this precious element of character on the one side or on the other. Certainly neither can claim its monopoly. It is the inestimable heritage of British religion; for we have had no Bartholomew, either of Huguenots or of Anabaptists, to destroy such a sanative. It was the head of the monarch and not the soul of the people that fell, while France and Germany chose the monarch at the people's cost. So that, in France, when the monarch did fall, there was no public conscience to be executioner. And in Germany it is the lack of a public conscience that has encouraged the imperial *Wahnsinn*, fed the ὕβρις, and inflated the pride that precedes a fall, whether in victory or defeat. Germany has been ruined morally and politically for want of Church freedom and its public courage. It is this Puritan note in church and chapel that is the differentia of our spiritual history, and also of our public. The moral note in our religion has been the soul and secret of our national liberty, our sympathy with liberty, and our service to it in the world. My only misgiving and complaint is that the tendencies of religious culture among us during the last two or three generations may have cut the communications by which this moral genius has been fed. The new humanism may have detached the general conscience of our national Christianity from the one public focus of moral creation and inspiration in the Cross of Christ—the Cross understood evangelically, as the crisis and regeneration of the universal conscience of the world by the eternal conscience of a God of holy love.

Such views of theology as postpone experience to belief, practice to creed, conscience to assent, or regeneration to impression, in the non-moral way I have named, are among the chief reasons why the Church has such a weak moral impact on the world, and why its theological foundations seem irrelevant to righteousness and impotent for crisis in history and society. They do not coincide with the foundations of the moral world. Therefore they are regarded as themes instead of being felt as powers. They are treated as academic principles instead of life-giving spirits. Such considerations help to explain why the Gospel of God's Kingdom (which, by right, is the one International) does not come home to the nations, why it does not take charge of the public conscience on a universal scale either to inspire courage or to sustain fortitude. They explain also how it is possible socially for evangelical sentiment to co-exist with commercial rapacity without a deadly jar; for the methods of the Standard Oil Company to share the enthusiasm of the same soul with Church life and Sunday-school work; and, generally, how men can lead a double life, and divide the one soul between the keen egoism of civilisation and the self-sacrifice of the Gospel, without feeling miserable or dishonest—till one day. One day the moral anomaly suddenly explodes, and the latent ethical outrage takes its natural and inevitable effect in a world war which but makes overt what was implicit in competition, besting, and tariffs. So the one Judge of all the earth does right. A religion which teaches men to live from two centres instead of one, and that one the conscience, is a non-moral religion; it serves God and Mammon. It has a fearful looking for of judgment. It has the soul of schism in it, which takes effect in the wars of churches, classes, and nations. War, with a national competition for God as ally, instead of a national obedience to Him as Sovereign, war with its eagerness to have Him on our side instead of having His side for ours, such war is but the debacle of a religion which is but sequentially, instead of essentially, moral, whose ethic is but a by-product. It is the fruit of the union of a civilisation which is fundamentally egoist, and a religion also egoist and propositional, sentimental, or what you will, only not holy. An egoist civilisation, an individualist salvation, and a non-moral theology in a world which belongs by right to the kingdom of conscience and God, and has that for its great deep *nisus*—such things do not make debacle strange or judgment wonderful. The shock would be if the combination did not so explode.

CHAPTER VI

THE FAILURE OF THE CHURCH AS AN INTERNATIONAL AUTHORITY

A TELEOLOGY of the world with a divine destiny for it in righteousness is so beclouded and belied by the actual course of events that the form in which revelation guarantees it must be (amongst other things) a theodicy. It must be a historic self-justification of God. And that must be not theoretical but historic—a practical establishment of His holy goodness in the face of everything. It must be something historic which enables us to believe in the last reality, deep rule, and final triumph of goodness in spite of history. This is no light matter, if we do not live in a cell or a balloon. It is not so hard to believe in a blessed teleology of the world by virtue of Christ's work and Word—till we come to know the world. Very much faith is only possible through ignorance of one's self, banality of standard, or lack of experience of the world. It is the confidence of those that have never had their self-confidence severely shaken. It is a faith which plain souls immune from wrong or innocent of guilt take for a hermitage. It was acquired by no taste of life's last tragedy, no real experience that challenged the justice of God; hence it is strange to the moral soul's last victory in the Cross. It may be the faith of people who take much culture, but never grow up, never pass beyond a pietist or an æsthetic religion. It is due to a sheltered existence, a happy temperament, a limited knowledge of life's bitterness and wickedness, and no knowledge at all of our own damnability. Nothing is to be said against such people until they propose their type of religion as standard for Christian faith, or definitive for the Gospel's crucial relation to the world. That would be a folly only matched by that of insisting at the other extreme that every Christian should pass through the tragic experience of a Luther. The weakness of the more idyllic type comes to light in the great crisis. When a sudden crash brings such people face to face with tragedy in its ghastliest and most inhuman forms, a faith which was only humane or serene in its note is apt to give way. It had but a divine atmosphere rather than a divine foundation. That the greatest and cruellest war in the world should take place between the two nations for which evangelical Christianity has done most, and to which its history owes most, would be serious for that form of faith if the Roman form had been capable of rising to the moral opportunity and taken the occasion to protest. It is a staggering blow to a faith that grew up in a long peace, a high culture, a shallow notion of history, society, or morality, and a view of religion as but a divine blessing upon life instead of a fundamental judgment and regeneration of it. It is fatal to the piety of pony carriage, shaven lawn, or æsthetic tea. Such an experience as the present cannot but mean very much for the whole public conception of the Church's word and function in the world. Can the Church give the ravaged and bewildered world a theodicy equal in power to the challenge? Or is its own faith but staggering on to its goal, with many falling out to die by the way? Is its God justified in expecting the trust and the control of a world which He has allowed to get into such a state? Has He gone deeper than its tragedy? Is the Cross He bore really a greater tragedy and monstrosity than war? The war is a greater misery and curse than we know, greater than we have imagination to realise—even if we had more facts for imagination to work on. Are we quite sure that it is a greater cross to God than to us, that it is but a part of the tragic and bloody course of history whose sword has pierced through His own heart also, and that His Redemption still is in command of all, and His Kingdom sure ? His insight misses nothing of all the facts and His holiness none of the horror ; does it unhinge Him ? Or is the Word of His Cross a vaster salvation than we dream, who are blinded by fears and tears, and whose conscience is not equal to conceiving either the enormity or the salvation ? Are the most prompt to speak the most penetrating in their grasp or the most potent in their effect ? One covets in wonder the faculty of simple solution, ready advice, and sweeping criticism in some.

One reads appeals made *sans gêne* by some whose measure of the situation is not equal to their good intentions, and who even give the impression of meeting the Atlantic with a mop. We come across machine-made appeals to the Church to be getting ready to handle the situation when the war is over. As if a Church which could not prevent its coming about would have much effect on the awful situation when it is done ! If the Churches so little gauged the civilisation which they had allowed to grow up, and which carried the war in its womb, are they more likely to grasp the case when the moral confusion is worse. If they were so impotent before, how are they going to be more powerful now ? What new source of strength have they tapped ? If the Church left such a war possible, what encourages us to think that it will discover the radical method by which 'a recurrence of these experiences may be rendered impossible' ? Democratic control ! Who or what is controlling or instructing the democracy ? The ideologues ? A parliament of blue birds ! If 'it has been shown how inadequate the influence of the Churches has been to restrain the forces of international strife,' it is not because the Churches have been inactive. They have been active even to bustle, not to say fuss. Is there something wrong or inept in the rear of their activity, in the matter of it, in their mental purview, spiritual message, and moral power. And is it more than fumbling with the subject to indulge in platform platitudes about 'wielding a universal influence over the actions not only of individuals but of the whole community of nations.' This kind of speech does something to depreciate the value of language, and to lighten the moral coinage.

The Gospel is not primarily and offhand a message of peace among men, but of peace among men of goodwill. If the amateur advisers of the Church will realise that its first work, which carries all else with it, is not to lubricate friction but to create among men that goodwill, to revise and brace the belief which has failed to do it, to think less of uniting the Church and more of piercing to a deep Gospel that will; if they will distrust the bustling forms of activity, the harder beating of the old drums, the provision of ever more buns and beverages; if they will court more the silent, searching, hateful regenerations that transform conduct, private and public, by a transformation of the faith that breeds Christian love and saves it from mere fraternity or comradeship—then they will be doing more than all the press, platforms, societies, or crusades can to aid the Church to acquire the moral influence it has confessedly lost. It is not clear that the minds whose words I quote believe in a judgment more than formally. It is not certain that they have real insight into its moral meaning and function. Judgment does not stir us up bravely to new activity till it has set us down humbly to new inquiry as to the causes of the old failure, as to the purpose and method of God which we have so failed to grasp. The Church reared the nations but it is not able to control them for the Kingdom of God. Why? What is missing in its message for adult peoples? Much political speculation is afloat as to the settlement among the nations after the war—most of it without data, and most of it leaving entirely out of account the most urgent matter of all, the matter of a real international power, integrating the peoples with moral and not merely political force. This is the place the Church should fill. If the Roman Church could do it, we need not mind the Romishness of it, which can be dealt with otherwise. But the Roman Church is itself, by its curialist ambitions, too much one of the worldly powers to mediate between them. It is too much of an empire for such emprise. And the other Churches are either too much nationalised, or too much rationalised, or too much sectarianised, or too atomic, and all too much divided, to possess this moral influence over and between the peoples, and to provide, not merely an arrangement, but an authority to give it effect. To repair this impotence is the first duty of the Church. And it simply shows an inability to gauge the situation to speak of the Church getting ready for influential action after the war. The statesmen will pay no attention to it. Nor should they, till it put its own house in order, realise anew its Gospel, and acquire from its own neglected resources the moral dignity and judgment, bold, serene, and august, which would save it from the busybodies and tittlebats to become the conscience of the world.

Nothing has more struck some than the lack of due and public reference to the Kingdom of God as the interest that any Christian nation must supremely serve for its permanent place in Humanity. We of this country have indeed much to answer for. Some of our greatest leaders and policies have been but pagan. Much of our conduct is still. But we remember that twice we have saved the liberty of the world—in the Armada, and at Waterloo. Have we become unworthy to do it again ? We sent forth the great free people of the West. There are those who think that Britain's record in such things as Slave Emancipation, Catholic Emancipation, the emancipation of the workman, the woman, and the child ; in the self-denying ordinance taking effect in the government of India by way of atonement for its acquisition ; in the treatment of South Africa since the Boer War, and especially of our enemies there (a treatment of which no other country than England was capable)—I say there are those who think that such and other like things show a growing repentance which only prigs could call Pharisaism, and a moral power which only pagans would call quixotic. These things place us in another class, so far as God's Kingdom goes, from a nationalism which is ostentatiously outside moral or humane regards, and is abetted by its Church in their neglect. We have at least begun to reverse our engines. The cause of the weaker nations has often owed us much. And if in the dark races our trade has been known to exploit and cajole, our Government has stepped in to protect and save. If we remember Bismarck and the falsified telegram, let us not forget Clive and the false treaty—except to reflect that Clive was not a national agent but the servant of a trading company, and by the House of Commons was disgraced.

Nor have we as a nation quite failed that word of God's truth and grace for which He cares above the fate of nations or the spread of culture. If there be a kingdom coming with all God's might to rule the earth, then, as nations go, Britain, by God's grace, has done more for it than most. We are at least on the way to serve God's Kingdom rather than extend our own. And this is our only ground of patriotic prayer ; which means patriotic humility, and some true compunction for what does not raise us above gross national egoism. We can pray for victory as a means to continue a service to that Kingdom which other nations have not yet given, and which cannot be given by mere aloofness, and neutrality, and a sense of moral superiority.

And yet, and yet. The present judgment is one upon a whole egoist and godless civilisation, of which we also are a part, and whose end is public madness. We too are not immune from the spirit of worldly Imperialism, of non-moral Nationalism, of passionate Mammonism, of Militarism, of the ideals of the Christless world masking often in a religious guise. And who can tell, when all is balanced in the scales of God, whether we are clean enough to hope to be continued in the service and course, which some hoped we had begun to lead, for His Kingdom on Earth. Let us speak of serving and not of deserving. Certain it is that, if the Kingdom of God be the active, historic, moral, and withal mystic and eternal thing the New Testament reveals, such neglect of it as modern society shows, and such repudiation of it as German nationality has deliberately made, must mean a judgment which our whole godless civilisation must feel, however we distribute the guilt. 'Both good and bad endure one scourge, not because they are guilty of one disordered life, but because they do both too much affect this transitory life ; not in like measure but both together.' (Augustine, *City of God*, i. 6.)

But this is a long excursion, not to say alarm. My point was that even the Church's grasp of the great moral teleology of history was not commanding; that it did not realise the sovereignty of the Kingdom of God for history ; that even where this was believed, it was too much mixed with pagan or humanist conceptions supremely to serve the purpose of God. And this because, owing to the Fatherhood ousting the Atonement, and the genial submerging the holy, salvation is not grasped in moral terms, as the theodicy of God, or His self-justification in righteousness, but only as a rescue from certain ills. It is understood egoistically with man as centre and not God. Desperate diseases, I have said, require desperate remedies. Extreme crises call for principles that may well seem extravagant to our peaceful hours. And there are plenty that will think it extreme to extravagance, and even to absurdity, when it is suggested that the first business of the Church to find its way in this world is to go back and recover its footing in another, to return and readjust its compass at the Cross, to rise above both the precepts and the principles Christ taught to the power He put forth there for the world's regeneration, and to recover a Christian ethic, not interim but final, there—at the seat of Christian judgment unto moral reconciliation. Is there any section of the Church that does not need to learn more deeply that the site of God's supreme revelation is not in the order of the world but in its crisis; that its nature is for the conscience not evolution but revolution; that it does not consecrate a natural ethic so much as redeem it; that by a new creation the Cross is both the foundation and the crisis of the whole moral world; that it was a tragedy greater and more searching than any war; and that it is the creative source of the new morality, the new Humanity? It is a far more free, flexible, and powerful ethic that is created by the new life of Christ, the Redeemer, than that promoted by the new precept of Christ the Seer.

This sounds like saying that a theological revision is the one thing the Church needs to regain control of the world. Well, there is a sense in which that is absurd; but in the deepest sense it is true, supremely true. God's answer to the world is to a world morally desperate, to the bankrupt conscience of the world. It is a dogmatic answer, as the way of conscience must be, which is the way of the moral imperative. Thou *shalt* love. It is an answer to our deepest need and not to our eager mind. It is certainly theological, though it is not necessarily systematic. It is the saving answer of the holy to the sinless. And it is much more than either simple or sweet. 'By terrible things in righteousness dost Thou answer us, O God of our Salvation.'

Many current conceptions of the Cross of Christ (both orthodox and heterodox) do not give it its due place as the creative focus of the moral world, and therefore as the rightful and the real ruler of the course of history. It does not appear as at once the solution and the destruction of the world's moral anomalies. In current belief there is a natural ethic and there is a Christian in a parallelism; and between them the conscience comes to the ground distracted and unsure. The latter—the Christian—is more or less optional, but the former is held to be vital for character and society. Hence the Christian morality is but one section of a divided soul. It is not the Church only that is divided; our conscience is. Our eye is not single. And therefore we cannot acquire the moral momentum necessary for a Christian control of great public issues. The centre of our religion is one thing, that of our morals another. We serve two masters. The great, the ecumenical morality is robbed of the sanction of faith and *élan* of eternity. And the great, the absolute, religion is demoralised. The Kingdom of God is treated as an interest which does not concern nations, but only missions and philanthropies. Policy may remain pagan if religion stands by with ambulances, lenitives, opiates. The Cross has for the heart a securing (I will not say always a saving) and consoling power, but it is not in the same position for active life. It belongs to personal religion only, and chiefly to what might be called the night side of that. It has the vespertinal note. It is not for political or business affairs. It has not the dimensions of history. The Cross is not felt to be the source of the eternal theodicy of time, the answer to human sin, wrong and misery, of a self-justifying God. Whereas if He spared not His own Son, all that seems merciless in the history of the world is less merciless than that, which is the shutting up of all men to mercy that neither falters nor repents.

As I am in some hope that these words may be read by my fellow-ministers, especially by the younger men amongst them, I have allowed myself to use some technical terms—although not without explanation in their immediate vicinity. Among such terms are the words anthropocentric and theocentric, whose meaning, I trust, I have not left obscure. They mean, much and very much, for our present frame of mind. Anthropocentric religion means egoist religion. It is religion whose God revolves on man. This has much social meaning. The state of a society is always chiefly and radically due to its religion; and I have been suggesting that the religion of current society has come to a serious pass and a day of judgment, because it has become anthropocentric, because it caters to individual or racial egoism, because it has come to regard God's love as the greatest asset of man instead of man's trustful obedience as the supreme worship and due of God. It has come to regard God as the patron of certain nations instead of viewing all the nations as vassals of the Kingdom of God. Or the Kingdom of God is understood as if He were the perpetual president and trustee of a human republic ruled by democratic ideas of which He has charge. The whole of civilisation has carried this egoist note into its religion, in so far as it remains religious and thinks of God at all. And, where it has ceased to be religious, it is partly because this note is incapable of holding and ruling so great a power as man now feels himself to be. If society is not duly religious, it is largely because its type of religion is unable, from its nature, to establish itself in command. All, as I say, comes back to the type of religion. The kind of religion is responsible for the ignoring of religion. A religious type which has abused, trivialised, and therefore desecrated, the idea of love by dropping from it the ideas of majesty, sovereignty, and judgment, is not one which can expect to keep the egoism of lusty man in its due place. A visitation of this royal Lord was well due. Nothing deserves or needs judgment so much as the neglect and contempt of judgment. And the only stable footing for any society is the theocentric note which first glorifies God and hallows His Name.

So I will put another shade of interpretation upon the word theocentric; I will say that it means the absolute supremacy of the holy. The bane of modern and current religion is in the practical loss of the idea so closely identified with Love's might, majesty, judgment, and glory—the idea of the holy. Either it is lost, or there is substituted for the moral meaning of it the æsthetic, and for the ethical the seemly; so that the response is but reverence instead of real worship, attrition instead of repentance, an extreme regard to religious decorum and good form (in the conduct of services, for instance), but no equal regard for the type and tone of life. There is not an equal regard for the way of life which keeps at its centre the holy as moral passion and mystic conscience, as the searching righteousness which enthrones God's love and destroys guilt in grace. I have seen congregations visibly relax attention when the preacher began to speak of the holiness of God. And the root of this error, which taints and flattens the whole field of religion, is the abeyance of an atonement as the foundation of our faith, the atmosphere of our worship, and the principle of our life. It comes to be treated as a theological arrangement in sequel to the Incarnation, instead of being the very nature, focus and function, of the Incarnation. This means, as I have said, that the moral is postponed to the metaphysical or the miraculous, and the whole tone of Christian life falls into that deadly tune. The one meaning of an atoning Cross is the securing and establishing of God's holy and righteous judgment throughout the moral world to its victory in love—His bringing forth judgment to such victory. It is the consummation of the holy conscience of God in the eternal action of love which incessantly creates a moral universe. If such an atonement become otiose to our faith (as is increasingly the case), the note of the holy, *i.e.* of the moral, must fade from it; and we are left with little beyond a piety either æsthetic, mystic, or sentimental, but too easy for judgment, too feeble for the control of civilisation, and fit only to become a branch of its culture. And the man of mere culture is shut out from the best it is in him to be.

It is to the religion of an age, that is, to its deep moral theology, that we must go back for the explanation of what befalls the age—it is not to its mere morality. The chief failure of Christianity is indeed a moral failure, a failure to become a guide for modern society, a curb and a cure for its godless egoism. But the root of the failure goes deep into a very spiritual kind of morality. The source and sublimate of the moral is the holy, which in God's righteous love is calling to man's warm conscience, to his moral heart, and calling for the whole man, the whole soul, the whole personality, and not merely a faculty of it, nor for its behaviour. It calls for the response known as faith, in which the personality assigns itself to the grace of the Holy in an act of committal which is holy as He is, and which has all actual sanctity latent in it, and all conduct. The act of each moment slumbers in the life of the doer seen whole as one compendious act. Such is the religion that answers Christian revelation. It is one compendious Act, into which the whole personality goes, responsive in kind to the one eternal Act in which the whole person of the Revealer takes standing effect as Redeemer. All the best history of the Church was latent in the Act of its salvation; and all the best in personal history and character lies hid in the act of faith wherein we pass from death to life. But nothing is more conspicuous in the popular Christianity now being shocked to its senses than the loss of the sense of the holy God amid the fair humanities of new religion, and the corresponding loss from faith of the sense that it is the grand and inclusive moral act of the personality; losses both which are vainly veiled by the mysticism that soothes so many. It is a loss that follows the retirement from Christian interest of the idea of a real Atonement, and the decay of the type of faith centring round it, *i.e.* the faith of the Cross as being, first and foremost, an offering of obedience to the holy will and judgment of God therein hallowed. God so loved the world, we read, that He gave His Son as a propitiation to His own holiness. He gave His holy Self in His Son. But God so loved the world, we are now taught, that He was not going to let His holiness interfere with its salvation. He had means to hush that holiness, or salve it, but we should not speak of satisfying it. Satisfaction is obsolete theology. At any rate He took it less seriously than His pity. But surely that is a non-moral creed, one which is but sympathetic, one therefore which must issue in an immoral society, first delightful then debased. Room must be made for a real judgment in any social salvation. It is quite inadequate to seek to fill from the Sermon on the Mount the moral vacuity which is left in the Cross when the Atonement there to a holy God has been taken away. Yet this is what current Christianity, with its centre on Incarnation and its plan with two natures rather than wills, tends to do. And it is why it is socially so sterile; it is ethically too inert and æsthetic. This atoning salvation is the only one that intrinsically moralises the *soul* itself by tuning it to the holy in the act of its rescue, and does not have morality as a mere sequel. And it is this moralising of the soul, behind all conduct or sentiment, that needs to be restored, if religion is to regenerate conduct or society. We need for society a religion that recreates the conscience, and does not simply enlighten or stimulate it. Do not, therefore, show up the inconsistencies of Christendom. Any youth can do that. Bear with all your strength on the centre of the soul where conduct rises and inconsistency fades. Turn all the moral creativeness of this Cross on that point. Bear upon the Christian regeneration of the *conscience* as the organ of the holy love, and therefore as the saviour of society from the unholy egoism of prosperity. Bear in on the public a Gospel that leaves a man with nothing to offer or say before a holy God, yet possessing all things in His holy grace. Do it with all the resources of culture and knowledge, with a generous heart and creed. But do it. The moral centre and future of society lies in the Cross of a holy Christ.

That is the one thing morally needful. It is the true line of moral reconstruction for Christianity at least. Yet there is a form of earnest religion which feels and is deeply Christian but which does not really rise above ethic and ethical criticism in its outlook on society. There is a type of pious reformer who is somewhat given to act the censor of the society round him, without the stamp of moral passion, and without such a grasp of the Gospel as makes its principle more incisive than the preacher can be. The impression left sometimes is that of a censor rather than of a judgment. And there is much risk, on this line, of developing a kind of critic who, even if we abstained from charging him with spiritual pride, should yet betray pride's accent of aloofness and self-will without pride's passion or power. Such criticism would have moral interests but no moral insight, spiritual fervour without discernment of spirits. It is self-sure if not self-righteous; it is but inchoate as an apostle—a disciple, but an apostle not yet. The temptation for such is great to describe the inconsistencies and crudities of a Christian society as Pharisaism, without any historic sense of what Pharisaism really was. The critic of Pharisaism may become a Pharisee without knowing it, and the Pharisaic type of mind is too egoist for a theodicy.

In a time of public crisis and peril the Church asks herself if she is in any way to blame (it is mostly too late then for her to save). And in this inquest she receives much help

There are plenty of people ready to expose, with considerable fidelity, with qualified sympathy, and with much publicity, the anomalies so easy to find in a lofty religion that covers large areas of people. Now we should not fail to recognise in the prophetic critic a great gift from above, to clear us of cant and phlegm. But let us not fail also to try his spirit, to discern it, and to criticise the critic for the authentic note and judgment of the moral seer. For impatience of evil is not moral judgment; indeed, it may destroy it; '*saeva indignatio perturbabat mentem.*'

There has often arisen in the name of conscience a type of reformer whose inspiration is unequal to his task, because he is more the censor of the unapt saints than the prophet of the righteous Lord. With the candour of the friend, he may be without the kindness of the brother; and with the mark of the ideal, he may be without the note of the apostle. He lacks the stamp of moral passion in the great style, moral imagination, the gift of insight into the last moral reality, or such a grasp of principle as makes it more incisive than the critic is. Such pietist criticism may have moral fervour, but no spiritual discernment, only sensibility. Mobility is taken for penetration, facility for real familiarity; and the sense of contrast is without perspective. Moral zeal, lost to a just sense of moral values, was very early seen to be a symptom of moral decay. It had no power to understand the weightier matters of the law, nor the insight that appraises moral principles in a hierarchy; it had not the flair for the Kingdom of God; and it was in its element among the lapses of the little.

For such minds it is not hard to impale a particular public scandal, or to collate several sets of incongruities from the moral life of a society which is only becoming Christian—as the critic himself may be but ethically adolescent. There is a certain amateur ethic, for instance, with more taste than faculty for public affairs, which brackets the gross sins of camps in a parity with the grisly sins of Cabinets, deadlier because subtler. It dubs as dishonest the society which admits the one within itself while denouncing the other elsewhere. It equates the non-respectable sins of popular instinct heat and haste, the vulgar sins, with the long, calculated, and diabolic wickedness of moral cynicism in the high places of genius or position. It brings to one level sensual and spiritual sin, sin haunted by a law it owns and sin which repudiates the existence of a law. It would slay with equal breath the secret indulgents of instinct and those more sinister corrosives who have been public idols for decades, and have spent their decent lives in cunningly seducing one nation to ravish another. It would tell us that because of the recent substitution, among women, workmen, and the aristocracy, of social terrorism for constitutional action, therefore it is dishonest to be so indignant about 'frightfulness' from abroad. And if such slovenly ethic be deprecated, if it is urged that a society has the duty while lamenting and mending the one to denounce and destroy the other—this is still trounced as Pharisaism. The temptation of those leonids who give way to that mood is to describe all the inconsistencies and crudities of a growing society as Pharisaism. The critics who never grow up are somewhat prompt with such language. And it is freely applied to our part in the war. Pharisaism is a handy word, a little shopworn now, but with many effective still; for we all hate a fraud. But it needs to be used with some care if it is to be more than censorious or priggish.

Pharisaism was not in its inception hypocrisy, as that word is promptly understood. It was a sect and a system which led there at the long last, but it did not begin there. It did not begin as conscious duplicity, but as unconscious unreality, as a disease not of the conscience but of the soul. It is not an ethical complaint but a religious. The Gospel judges the world, but it was the religious that Jesus judged. The very quarrels of religion, the divisions in the Church, are due to the sound conviction that nothing can be so fatal to religion as wrong religion. Pharisaism turned radically on the religious treatment of its central sanctity, and not on the moral adjustment of conduct to principle. Its malady was, first, the anthropocentrism of which I have spoken. It elevated man (or a nation) and exploited God. It had use for God only in so far as He was committed to the glorification of Israel. And, second, as a consequence of this, it courted for itself the eminence in the religious community which it claimed for that community in mankind. Its note was not first false religion but superior religion, higher spirituality, advanced ethic. It cherished the note of conscious superiority in its religious style, a superiority which lay not in repentance but in spiritual attainment and a company of choice and separate spirits. So it became unreal. And its temper remains to this day. It is a false form less of conduct than of sanctity. It is less inconsistent conduct than self-conscious sanctity, which takes itself as seriously as its salvation. A touch of humour would sometimes reduce it, if it did not cure it. It is the crime of a religious society, and not of a natural, of Church rather than State, and it is a temptation to the leaders of such society especially. It besets religious coteries and sects. And it aims there at special spirituality and a laboured or mannered holiness, whether in the way of observance or of experience. It is not moral inconsistency, therefore, professing one thing and living another, so much as it is conscious, superior, censorious, and therefore spurious religion. It is apt to affect those better spirits who covet holiness; and it tends to attack especially those who have laid themselves out to be spiritual influences. It is an insidious disease, and not a devised fraud. It can be more deadly than fraud, since it is less easily found out; being honest self-delusion about reality, about God, on the part of people who take religion for a career and who work at being good.

It is not Dickens's Pecksniff but George Eliot's Bulstrode (in *Middlemarch*). But then Dickens was a sentimental moralist of the obvious and extravagant type, who made hypocrisy strut for our amusement, while George Eliot was a sympathetic prophet, who got inside it, and let us see the pitiful growth of its slow perdition for our warning. It is worst among the earnestly religious, for whom religion is a life and does not simply fill up certain gaps in life. It was, in the classic form, the evisceration of religion by people intensely devoted to it, people, indeed, more concerned about the piety of their religion than about the truth of their revelation, people engrossed with holiness but spending more on the cultivation of their own than on the understanding of God's. It is devoted, subjective, and even egoist piety, at the cost often of moral judgment. It could even, in extreme cases, be what many a cloister has seen—the ambition of sanctity, instead of the habitual and hearty confession of repentance, with the love of fellow-sinners long before they attain to saints. It is in danger, in such conditions, of substituting elated religion for humble faith, visionary exaltation for broken trust, calm eminence for kind courtesy, and that for frank fraternity. It tends to take spiritual aptitude for evangelical trust, and to overlay the work of the holy upon the conscience by the mystic glamour of temperament, or the æsthetic spell of religious culture. Perhaps the best practical commentary on it is the history of monasticism, from its beginning in earnest spirituality, through strained, then through fantastic, piety, to moral erosion and collapse.

Those do us a true service, therefore (if they are careful), who warn us against Pharisaism ; who go back to the first Pharisaism, to discover that the Antichrist in it was deepened by the Christianity in it ; and who teach us that the first falsity was the substitution of religion for God, of spiritual attainment for searching humility ; of an egoist piety for a sympathetic faith with the self-distrust of one whose foot nearly slips. We need constantly to be told that, for all the higher purposes of religion, quality is a greater matter than intensity, that it is of more moment that God's name should be hallowed than spread. So, if we may gather up the best teaching on the subject, we note, first, that Pharisaism is a religious vice rather than an ethical. Second, that it begins, not as hypocrisy, but as unreality, as religious unreality which (through a dread of theology) is so subjective that it never suspects how unreal it is. It is unconscious humbug long before its issue in obvious quackery. We note, third, that it is apt to attack the spiritual rather than the average man. Its bacillus thrives rapidly in the high and exposed places of religion, in eminent Christians (as the phrase used to be). Fourthly, the attack may be most severe in these unworldly souls who are sensitive to a Kingdom of God, and who set out to cultivate spiritual influence among the young or crude, not for love of power but as a lever for good. Pharisaism of this kind was one of the temptations of Christ from the best religion of His day. 'Get power with the public by religion that impresses them ; then use it for a great reign of righteousness.' Such people are not self-seekers in the vulgar sense. They do not fall to spiritual pride, which is too Satanic and thorough for their natures, but to what may be called spiritual 'side,' with pride's accent of self-certainty, remoteness, and *de haut en bas*, but without its passion or power. And, fifthly, as it seizes on the religious, it is the more dangerous with those who take their religion most seriously, who not only feel the spell of the spiritual but cultivate it as some writers do style. The result may be similar too. There is a spiritual preciosity—as there is a literary—both unreal, and both on the slope that ends in self-sophistication. It is dangerous to cultivate piety for our uplifting when we need to be acquainting ourselves with God for our peace ; for spirituality is much easier than repentance. And in subjective sanctity we are thought by men to be doing something, whereas we seem to them but theologising when we are lost in the holiness of God; and then it takes so much time. Thus it is that we suffer from the *blague* about the need of religion instead of theology. If it come to that, the Pharisees were more religious than the first disciples; and it was a matter of theology that separated them from Christ. They did not lack the sacrificial spirit. Like Him, they were quite ready to die for their nation's God. But they had a different view of God and His will. They were experts and veterans in sacrifice, but not according to knowledge. They worshipped it for its own meritorious sake. The case was not disobedience on one side and obedience on the other; it was a question of the kind of God who should receive an obedience taken seriously on both sides. They differed, not on what was due to revelation, but on what came by it.

Pharisaism, in a word, was Antichrist because it was anthropocentric religion. For it God's Kingdom must glorify Israel, while for Christ it must glorify God. Other nations might save themselves, God alone could save Israel, said Christ. God does not wait on man's aspirations or ambitions, man is there to worship God's glory. Christ was little moved by a religion of moral excellence, such as many a Pharisee successfully pursued. He was all for a religion of salvation, in which the penitent went for more than the excellent. And the faith of the Cross means that history is not run solely or primarily in the interest of mere moral worth, but in the interest of Redemption, and of the holy judgment that goes with redeeming Love's right to all men, not its mere value for them. God is not the world's great asset but its eternal Lord. And Pharisaism, as the great egoism, makes no theodicy possible.

To move the centre of supreme concern from God to

man is false religion, whose nemesis is slow but sure. Whether we do it in the pursuit of personal spirituality, public influence, or public prosperity, yet to nurse reputation, to cultivate people in order to do them good, instead of doing them good by loving them for God's sake, it is to surrender along with veracity the idea of the holy. It often entails spiritual overstrain, restlessness, and vagrancy. We may lose the power of the holy in a weak ethic which really cuts the moral nerve, and debases charity into a saltless sacrifice. The holy has no meaning apart from the conscience, majesty, and kingship of the righteous Father. Nor has the moral any ultimate meaning apart from the holy. And without the supremacy of the moral interest there is no path through history, no teleology of society, no theodicy. Without holiness no man shall see the Lord in history. To make the development of man the supreme interest of God, as popular Christianity sometimes tends to do, instead of making the glory of God the supreme interest of man, is a moral error which invites the only treatment that can cure a civilisation whose religion has become so false—public judgment. It is of more moment, I have said, that God's love should be hallowed than spread. God can spare us no judgment which is needful to *hallow* His love, and lift it from the fondness of a blind parent to the power which moves to His end the earth, the heavens, and all the stars. A society whose God, in whatever kindness, is less than holy represents in the end a godless civilisation; which must sink to moral hebetude, not to say moral monstrosity, even amid strong passions and lively affections; with a fearful looking for of the judgment which is at once the moral nemesis and the gracious cure. Man's holiness is not spiritual eminence, nor mystic remoteness, nor religious facility; it is moral insight and practical experience of love's miracle of majesty and mercy combined only in an atoning Cross. It is a perception of the conscience, and it acts on the conscience as nothing else does; it is therefore especially destined for public ethic on the scale of a new world. Religion, in losing the note of the holy, and its supremacy, loses the note of authority, which, in the end, is to lose all. And some Churches have quite lost it. And so they lose men. What a craving there is for this note, how far the sympathies and pieties which bring the hour's boon are from satisfying us, is shown by the extraordinary rally to the nation's army of our youth, which the Church had so freely lamented its inability to capture or to hold, of which it therefore was apt to despair. That rush to the ranks is not due to patriotism alone, but partly also to a resentment of the dull and soulless routine of the egoist civilisation to whose service most of their hours were bound without scope or hope. They welcomed a devotion. And, without authority, no devotion. The passion to be commanded, to obey, to sacrifice co-exists with the passion of insubordination and rebellion. Both Jesuitism and the Salvation Army have been created upon the recognition of this fact. And the distinction and attraction of obedience and service has been a great recruiting motive. The voluntary devotion to a great entity like country has done something to fill the moral gap left by the subsidence of the idea of a holy, majestic, commanding God from the heart of a religion of love, and by the disappearance from several Churches of a machinery of obedience. It shows how the personality, the soul, seeks, for its own dignity and completion, more than the 'heart' can give it. 'Why,' you ask, 'Why does the Church not win from youth the devotion that the nation wins?' Partly because the Church as popular is not offering a God or a Christ great enough to command life and conscience, and therefore to tap its devotion, but only near enough to promote sympathy. Partly because in some of its forms it not only does not provide, but it discourages, the obedience which is better than sacrifice and inspires it. We have been trying to cultivate sympathy faster than we provided an inspiration of sacrifice. The old-fashioned convert, whose conscience played the chief part in his change, and who parted with himself before he sacrificed his enjoyments, was more heroic in his note. A Gospel of kind love alone defeats its own end. Sympathy alone will not cure *for the soul* the egoism it resents in society, sacred or profane. And its obtrusion may repel the manlier breed.

It is the godlessness of civilisation in its two extremes of humanism and savagery, its egoist foundation and content even in its religion—the outrunning of moral progress by civilised—that is the source of its present downfall. And no theodicy can meet the situation which does not see that the root of the trouble is in some fundamental dislocation in the whole of society, however it may come to a head in a particular nation. The anomaly is not that a God of love should permit such things as we see. In the egoist conditions of Europe and of civilisation everywhere, and with a God of holy love over all, the scandal and the stumbling block would have been if such judgments did not come. We could not feel the world was in righteous hands. If only the chief culprits were the chief victims! But they are well entrenched in the sense of power, and even of justice. There is sent them a strong delusion. The worst curse, we have said, is not conscious hypocrisy, which is easily seen and soon found out. It is the deadlier element in Pharisaism, it is religious superiority, the superstition either of a pious *élite*, or a chosen and monopolist race, such as the Kaiser holds Germany to be. It is the absolute self-delusion which ends in moral madness, because it shrinks, beyond everything else, from a habitual self-reference to the Cross as the judgment-seat of Christ, and a constant correction there. Christ's servants, and not His comrades, we are, His property by heavenly purchase, and not simply His poor relations nor His weak allies. A religion whose ethic is not founded in its forgiveness, which is not a daily repentance but a constant self-satisfaction, and which only abets by sanction the passion for power of unredeemed man, is a daily invitation of judgment. And we are now learning what judgment is. We have descended into hell.

CHAPTER VII

TELEOLOGY ACUTE IN A THEODICY

THE faith of a teleology in history protects us from the vagrancy of soul which dogs the notion that things are but staggering on, or flitting upon chance winds over a trackless waste. It saves us from the timidity which so easily besets us before the incalculable. But our worst trouble is not due to a mere tracklessness in the course of history. That is too negative to try us keenly. We are exposed to positive assault. The iron enters our soul. The worst question rises, and the chief protest, when the disorder in the world touches our nerve in the shape of positive pain, evil, or guilt; when our personal life is deranged by that alien invasion, or is crushed, instead of stayed, by our connection with the course of things; when conscience rises in protest at the fate of the good, or the falsity of ourselves. Questions then come home about the connection of evil and suffering, sin and sorrow, grief and goodness. Then it is that the desire for a teleology quickens and deepens into the passion for a theodicy. Has the teleology a moral end? Is God's goodness secure? The teleology of things is congested into a crisis which demands that revelation be the self-justification of God. Is the great end not only there but is it just, and does it justify the dreadful means? Our quest for a divine plan becomes a concern for the divine justice. A God that merely hides Himself may, as Bacon says, be but playing hide-and-seek with His children, and longing to be found. He is more tolerable than one who is indifferent—much more tolerable than one who seems to withdraw offended to His heavenly tent when His creatures most need Him in their battle; or who even from His invisible retreat shoots casual darts upon them, or wraps them in a blight without sympathy or justice. The last demand of the soul is Job's—that God would vindicate his ways to men. We are more concerned that God should do justice to Himself than even to our hopes. For the time at least the religious interest of people has passed away from God's justification of man; it is all to the good therefore that it should fasten, in the growing strain of life, with the more force upon His justification of Himself. How should He expect us to trust Him, for instance, after a war like this, and a history of the race in keeping with it?

If our problem is Job's, the historic answer has now gone much further than what he received. The Cross of Christ has come and gone; and we do not simply bow with Job under a sublime majesty more sure and impressive than the mercy. But in the Cross of Christ as is His majesty so is His mercy. That is to say, He is gracious with all His might, and not in an arbitrary interval of His power. The solution there to the question of a teleology is not simply a *tour de force* of revelation; it is a moral victory and redemption; it is *the* moral victory which recovered the universe. The Vindicator has stood on the earth. It is the eternal victory in history of righteousness, of holiness, of the moral nature and character of God as Love. It is therefore the solution also to the teleological question in its more pointed form, as to a theodicy. It justified not man merely but God. The divine destiny of the world was not simply revealed in Christ but secured; and in a way which not only respected the holiness of God, but put it into action and leading action. The solution is equally religious and moral, as the Christian idea of the holy must be. It is evangelical, with the note of guilt, tragedy and glory. It is soteriological. It is a matter of judging grace, and of grace *taking* judgment. It is in the faith of God as a holy Saviour, and our deliverance from guilt in His Cross, Judgment, and Resurrection. God's justification of man opens our eyes to His justification of Himself. Both are one and the same act. The power of God unto salvation is the revelation and the energy of the righteousness of God (Rom. i. 16–17). It is holy love at work in final judgment, *i.e.* in the rectification of all things. The Cross of Christ creates in faith the assurance that the whole course of the world which entailed it is, before everything else, the explication of His work—a vast means for man's separation from his sin and union with his God. And thus by the Will and Act of God history fundamentally and finally serves His purpose of holy love. If it all seem very slow, and justice seem for periods even turned backwards, that only means that, since we do not see sin as God sees it, we have misconceived the problem. Those who are disappointed with the social success of Christianity must challenge the action of any beneficent power in history to the same extent. But, further, it is not *beneficence* but holiness that makes God God, and prescribes His action with the moral soul, with its intractability at worst, and at best its docility instead of its repentance. The most anomalous thing, the most poignant and potent crisis that ever happened or can happen in the world, is the death of Christ; the whole issue of warring history is condensed there. Good and evil met there for good and all. And to faith that death is the last word of the holy omnipotence of God. There is nothing hid from the light of His grace there, and nothing outside its service, its ethic, and its final mastery. The whole world is re-constituted in the Cross as its last moral principle, its key, and its destiny. The Cross is at once creation's fatal jar and final recovery. And there is no theodicy for the world except in a theology of the Cross.

The only final theodicy is that self-justification of God which was fundamental to His justification of man. No reason of man can justify God in a world like this. He must justify Himself, and He did so in the Cross of His Son.

No reason of man can justify God for His treatment of His Son; but whatever does justify it justifies God's whole providence with the universe, and solves its problem. He so spared not His Son as with Him to give us all things. The true theology of the Cross and its atonement is the solution of the world. There is no other. It is that or none. And that theology is that the Cross is not simply the nadir of Incarnation, but that it is God's self offering (under the worst conditions that love could feel for evil man) to His own holy name. The just God is the chief Sufferer and sole Doer. The holy love there is in action everywhere. The most universal thing in the universal Christ is His Cross. Everywhere, according to God's ubiquity, immanence, or what you will, His holy love is invincibly at issue with death, sin, and sorrow. Everywhere is redemption. And that is the only theodicy. The purpose of salvation is the principle of creation; and the ruling power of the world is the purpose of God.

It is no light problem that faces the Creator in His world. There was never such a fateful experiment as when God trusted man with freedom. But our Christian faith is that He well knew what He was about. He did not do that as a mere adventure, not without knowing that He had the power to remedy any abuse of it that might occur, and to do this by a new creation more mighty, marvellous, and mysterious than the first. He had means to emancipate even freedom, to convert moral freedom, even in its ruin, into spiritual. If the first creation drew on His might, the second taxed His all-might. It revealed His power as moral majesty, as holy omnipotence, most chiefly shown in the mercy that redeems and reconciles. To redeem creation is a more creative act than it was to create it. It is the last thing omnipotence could do. What is omnipotence but the costly and inevitable action of holiness in establishing itself everywhere for ever. The supreme power in the world is not simply the power of a God but of a holy God, upon whose rule all things wait, and may wait long. It is no slack knot that the Saviour has to undo. All the energy of a perverse world in its created freedom pulled on the tangle to tighten it. And its undoing has given the supreme form to all God's dealing with the world. But at the same time the snarl is not beyond being untied. Man is born to be redeemed. The final key to the first creation is the second; and the first was done with the second in view. If moral freedom is the crown of the first creation, spiritual, holy freedom is the goal of moral; and it is the gift in the second creation. The first creation was the prophecy of the second; the second was the first tragically 'arrived.' There was moral resource in the Creator equal to anything that might happen to the creature or by him. And that resource is put forth in Christ—in His overcoming of the world on the Cross, and His new creation of it in the Spirit. All God's omnipotence is finally there. The great goal is not the mere fruitage of the first creation, but another creation more creative still. The first does not glide into the second; there is a crisis of entirely new departure.

This was a salvation in which God first justified Himself, hallowed His own name, and made His eternal purpose good in those heavenly places which rule earthly things. His holy love is not there just as the instrument of man's salvation, but man's salvation is there to the glory of God's holy love. Man is only saved by God's holiness, and not from it, not in spite of it. He is saved by the tragic action of a holy God, by the honour done by God in Christ to His own holy name and purpose. There is a brief phrase in Julian of Norwich which has a whole theodicy in it: 'God will save His Word.' He is true to false man because first true to His own nature and promise. His justification of man is only possible by a practical justification of Himself. We should be more sure of man's salvation if we sought first God's righteousness—as He Himself does—if we were more concerned to secure His Kingdom than man's weal. There is nothing so good and wholesome for man as the Kingdom of God and its holiness, which Christ sought first, and won. Nothing else assures man's destiny, or realises all that it is in him to be. The great and final assurance we need is that God will save, must save, has saved His own holy purpose, gospel, and glory; and that history is the action of that salvation, surely however obscurely, irresistibly however slowly. With that faith we are sure of man's future. And only so. Man could never come to himself till God came to His own. If we first hallow God's name, as Christ did first, as God in Christ did, we are delivered from all evil, and all things are ours.

There is nothing so precious in the world as souls. All things are there for the rearing of holy persons, holy souls. And it is the goal of such personality that is the solution of the world—by the power over the world and the action in it of the living, loving God, whom Christ hallowed and trusted even when He spared Him not. Holy souls are so precious in the world because they carry the note of a holiness above the world, they are earmarked for it, and their destiny is the image of God. But Christ was not destined for this image; He wore it from the first. It was his own. He was and *is* the holiness of God. Therefore God in Christ, crucified and risen, under and over the world's worst sin, is His own theodicy. He is doing entire justice to His holy name. Christ stills all challenge since He made none, but, in an utter darkness beyond all our eclipse, perfectly glorified the Holy Father. If He, the great one conscience of the world, who had the best right and the most occasion in all the world to complain of God for the world's treatment of Him—if He hallowed and glorified God's name with joy instead (Matt. xi. 25–7; Luke xxiii. 46), there is no moral anomaly that cannot be turned, and is not by long orbits being turned, to the honour of God's holy love, and the joy of His crushed and common millions. His wisdom is justified of His children.

If this seem extravagant (and to many disciplined minds I fear it would if it reached them) may I again remind you that it is the large utterance that fits the consciousness of the Church, and it may well be too much for individuals who are Churchmen either not at all or but in part. We are now in a crisis that no individual can measure, nor his piety deal with; and it is beyond any philosophy or idealism of a time. It needs the faith of an agelong holy Church to grasp it. Would that the Church's faith could always handle it in the true power of that crisis greater still which made the Church—in the power of the Church's Cross and Gospel. An awful crisis of wickedness like this war can only be met on the Church's height and range of faith; and it forces us up to levels and aspects of our belief which our common hours of moral slackness too easily feel extreme. Nothing but the great theologies of redemption are adequate to the great tragedies of the world.

It is the triumph of Hellenic and philosophic wisdom to think that 'it is as wise to moderate our belief as our desires.' But with Christian wisdom it is not so. We cannot love God too much, nor believe too much in His love, nor reckon it too holy. A due faith in Him is immoderate, absolute trust, and it has a creed to correspond. Only an immoderate belief is true enough for the extraordinary tragedy of the world—the kind of belief in which Christ conquered the whole crisis of the world, not to say of Eternity. We are put upon no such trial of our faith as befell Christ. All our concern is but sectional compared with His. And no language is extreme which does justice to His conquest of His trial as the Act in which God's grace subdues the whole evil of the whole universe for ever. If that is not true there is no theodicy of the world, and in the end no teleology. We are still groping; and in our groping giving the lie to Christ, who was entirely holy, and perfectly sure of His own work as cosmic and final. What happens to the sinful creatures of God, however vastly tragic, is less monstrous than what happened to the Son of God. But what was done by the Son of God is, and He knew it to be, beyond all measure of speech or thought, above anything that God's children can do to each other of weal or woe. Not to realise this is to have less than the Christian insight, and another scale of values. All the great theologies are but poor efforts to pierce that heaven of the Cross, or to drop into that deep a plummet, which may register true, but will only sink so far and no further into the abysmal pressure. Christ finished the world-work given Him to do. He brought the world home. (If this was not the work given Him He was a megalomaniac, for He believed it was; and He infected His Apostles.) In Him the whole creation does but praise, laud, and magnify in advance the God of its salvation, evermore calling Him holy whatever has come and gone, and owning that it was worth all it endured to serve with such praise. Yea, it would go through it again at the Father's will. In Him the whole creation sees of the travail of its soul and is satisfied. He who can take away the sin of the world has in His reversion the reason, completion, peace, joy, and glory of all things. The Destroyer of guilt pacifies all grief, the Reconciler of our enmity ends all question. To see the devastator a truly penitent thief would compensate any Christian victim. The Justifier of men is the one and only theodicy of God. The Gospel, which is the power of God unto a soul's salvation, is so as the supreme action of the righteousness of a loving God with the whole world.

The world does not ask the question as it is put by the Church. The Church, starting from the Holy One, asks how man shall be just with that God, and she owes her existence to the answer in Christ's Cross and Gospel. But the world, with its egoist start, asks how God shall be just with man. The one brings man to God's bar, the other brings God to man's. Christ deals with both. The first question He answers with God's free justification of man, the second question He makes us recast. He does not bring God to man's bar but to God's own, since there is none greater. He brings God's providence to the bar of God's own promise, His own Gospel. He attunes it to God's own conscience, His own nature; He embodies the self-justification of God. In Christ we are justified freely by God's grace because God is fully justified by Himself; He bears Himself His holy judgment of the world. Is that too absurd to be true, is it too good to be true? If any man thinks he has anything to suffer in the flesh, God more. In all their afflictions He was more afflicted. The crime of man to man inflicts a greater wrong on God, *i.e.* on one who by His holy love is much more sensitive than man, and yet also more committed to do justice. God has more to carry in the Cross of His Son than man has in the nemesis of his sin. For God has to bear what sin means to the Holy, and not to a vision bleared by guilt, or a heart hardened by it past feeling. And that is something greater than all the catastrophe of time, on the principle that man is greater than the universe which crushes him, because he knows it. Christ in justifying man bore the last judgment of the world, seeing and feeling sin as the Holy alone does. But it is only those who are justified with God that know this self-justification of God, and His hallowing in Christ of His own holy name on the scale of the whole race. The justified do not challenge the justice of God. But for either philosophy or common sense this way of regarding things is an entire revolution. To see a world like ours as the process of a foregone and finished salvation is a change so prodigious and miraculous that it implies a change in us so great as passing from death to life. The last theodicy is our regeneration, which makes credible the new birth of the world whereof the soul is an organic part. This is the standing miracle; which is inadequately divined by those who think to solve the miracle question by saying vaguely that all is miracle, but who mean no more than that all is marvellous. The fundamental miracle is the new creation of creation by the grace of the Holy. It is not grace simply; for mercy alone is not so supernatural, but it is the grace *of the Holy*, the contact and embrace of sinners by the Holy. That is the miracle at the root of all Christian reality; for the sake of which all other miracles exist; and it is one which God alone could explain.

The chief bane of current religion, the loss of miracle, awe, and wonder, from its sense of love and tone of worship, is due to its neglect of the holiness of God; as if it were but a theological theme compared with His love, and one which might be relegated to the attention of those circles that discuss the divine attributes. Whereas it is no attribute unless love is. It is the first thing in God, His very being. His love is divine only because it is holy, and not because it is intense or wide; it is victorious and eternal only as holy, only as the Father is King in righteous majesty, mystic and infinite. God's holiness is the absolute monarchy of His righteous love. This popular dislocation of the holiness and the love of God, to the comparative neglect of holiness, or its relegation to a remote communion with Him by temperamental saints, means the unmoralising of love; and it is the cause of that loss of moral strength which robs the Church's message of its public influence; reduces it to the region of the individual, the mystic, the domestic, or the philanthropic; makes it sentimental bustle or else banishes it to an æsthetic worship where it is more revered than realised; and deprives it of power to reconcile either man with man, people with people, or history with God.

After all, the present cataclysm is an acute condensation of what has been going on in nature, human and other, for millenniums. If faith could survive that, need it succumb to this? If the existence of hell is compatible with faith in God, and is even of His ordinance, must we lose faith when it comes through earth's crust in a volcano? That is quite so. But two things aggravate the present crisis. Of one I have spoken—the shock of a Christian nation repudiating even natural ethic. The other is the violent disillusion of our hopes from civilisation. Yet is it so surprising? I have hinted more than once, that, for all its crushing effect upon the faith of many, the present disaster is less surprising when we read with the moral intelligence the tendency of things for a whole century and especially a whole generation. The dirty chimney needed to be fired. This flare has been long smouldering. Most of the drifts, and all the dominants, in modern civilisation were inviting it. Indeed, if it is hard to believe in a theodicy with things as they are, it would be harder still to trust Christian righteousness if disaster did not follow from things as they have been. The present situation a monument to the failure of the Church! Why, it is the necessary reaction on an egoist civilisation of the God of the Church's Gospel. The war is a revelation of man's evil on the one hand and God's righteousness on the other. In antiquity it must have seemed bewildering to the average Jew that Babylon should have been allowed to take away place and name from the nation that stood alone in the world for the true God. It destroyed the faith of most of them. But it brought out the prophets, to whose anointed eyes it was not a strange thing. The strange thing would have been if judgment had not come.

For judgment begins at the house of God, and the greater the light the greater the perdition. The people's treatment of their light in their prophets, the contempt for the preachers who ingeminated judgment in ears deaf to them but alert to all the false prophets, platforms, journals and politics of the hour—that could have but one end, if God's kingdom, righteousness, and humanity still endured. No culture can avert the judgment that always waits upon scorn of obedience and the contempt of law. No power can prevent the collapse of the hybristic mind. And civilisation, in capital and labour, male and female, young and old, has with us all been resenting submission to moral control, ousting conscience, slighting law, hailing revolt, cultivating violence, and reducing religion to a social decorum, where it was not driving the supernatural out of life. Its very ethic was attempted on an antitheological, not to say an unmoral, basis. Utilitarianism, organisation, efficiency were coming to rule all. The very rebels against law found their strength in combination, which is but law in another form. It was therefore inevitable that the vitality, the will, the personality, and all that goes with the voluntarist, active, creative side of man, the side where faith lives, should react, revolt, and claim its own against ubiquitous organisation. This has happened in the protest of the nations against the world empire of the one nation which itself had become the chief example of machine-made society, of the death of public opinion, and the denial of religious control. If there was to be room for the soul and a gospel for life at all it could not be a gospel of law, which is a contradiction in terms. The function of a gospel is to deliver us from law; not, however, by despising and abolishing it but by teaching it its beneficent limit and place. That place is not control. Neither law nor thought, no system of any kind, can take the supreme control of a person or society of persons without provoking revolt. Yet control there must be. And the friction of the time has been caused by the effort to control the initiative soul by a mere regulative system, to replace the moral order by material or intellectual organisation. The protest against law is made by the personality of mankind, which law was stifling, the State suppressing, and reason subduing to mere process. The German military system is like the rest of civilisation for the moment—an organisation of colossal forces handled by mediocre personalities. Whereas the chief assertion of power is an assertion of personality. But even then, even with a Napoleon, without moral control and loyalty, personality is but another and more dangerous force, increased by combination. What is to control, and harness, and develop personality? Not its organisation, either as a union or a nation. Only personality, only the action within it and over it of another Personality whose right it is to reign, only the action of the personal God, whose holy majesty is revealed in the imperative of conscience and its re-creation. But in the retreat of law, and the failure of Agnosticism, their place has been taken by a vast, vague Monism, whose action is not in the way of control but of increased impulse, and which is a mere dynamic overriding and erasing moral values in a civilised barbarism. It has more mass than quality; it is impressive but not authoritative; it affects but it does not command. Monism but feeds the assertive personality with new assertion. It abets the egoism which resents control. It makes it an orifice of the total world substance, process, and pressure in one individual direction. It puts behind the egoism all the force and sanction of a *natura naturans*. 'Be yourself, superhuman! Be all it is in you to be. Widen the outlet in you of mighty nature. Realise your individuality with unfaltering force and courage. Be afraid only of fear or weakness. Get in first, stay in last.' Nothing qualitative is here put over the Ego. It goes on till it run against a quantitative superior, a superior force of its own kind, a more energetic and demonic Ego, a greater degree of the universal *élan*. And that is not control, it is mere collision, with survival of the strongest, the most heartless, the most conscienceless will. For moral control we must have another person within the person, a conscience other but not alien to our own, a moral power which by a creative invasion changes the quality of the *élan*, and does not simply augment its volume or cross its path. There is no control in Monism with its force, law and efficiency, but only in Monotheism with its will, conscience, and love. We cannot indeed go back to Victorian legalism and rationalism. Yet to go forward to the action of a mere monistic world process is to go down. We can go on and up only if the growing sense of personal power and faculty in the race includes the witness in conscience and history to a personal Lord and God, who will spare us nothing, will spare not even His Son in His blood (which is Himself), that righteousness may reign and holiness cover the earth. The worship of law had to go, for law's own sake, but it has been replaced by no worship. We do not follow a lead, we are but borne on a stream. The growing sense of our own personality has been captured by no new sense of a sovereign personality, an imperative more sovereign, because more searching and humbling, than laws could be for a being intrinsically spiritual. Religion, which has grown indeed as a sensibility (as the taste for mysticism shows), has lost as a control. In a time of swelling power it has not grown as a power but only as an atmosphere. It has become fine for the few instead of powerful with the many, soft where it should have been strong to cope with the unprecedented egoism of the race. And we have in the whole moral situation what I have said we have in the war—the spectacle of colossal forces handled by mediocre personalities, forceful enough but not great. We have the reign of stupid ability, which can work its powerful engine, but cannot take the measure of a moral world, or even a political.

And what I am suggesting from the viewpoint of a theodicy is that, if righteousness remain, there could remain for such a situation but judgment, that the wonderful thing is not the judgment but its delay, that the amazement would be if no judgment did come. The surprise would be if everything went on in a godless civilisation as if men were waiting on the Lord instead of using Him to wait on them. But is there such a world righteousness in supreme and final command ? My case is that there is no certainty of it till we are sure of more. We cannot trust a world righteousness till we are sure of God's holiness. And the certainty of that is a matter of religion, and of atoning and redeeming religion. It is *the* matter of religion, the matter of *the* religion, of religion equally moral and mystic, of evangelical religion, of faith in the final crisis and victory of the moral soul, God's and man's, in the Cross of Christ, who has overcome the world for good and all in an eternal Act of love, judgment, grace and glory. He starts the new ethic in creative mercy, the new Humanity in regenerative forgiveness ; and the forgiveness has its moral ground in atonement to the living law, to the holy God, the God of the whole moral universe, and of the Church in so far as the Church is the earnest of a whole and holy world. The Cross is not a theological theme, nor a forensic device, but the crisis of the moral universe on a scale far greater than earthly war. It is the theodicy of the whole God dealing with the whole soul of the whole world in holy love, righteous judgment, and redeeming grace. There is no universal ethic but what is based in that power and deed. There is no sound theology but what moves in universal righteousness to a universal Kingdom of peace and joy to the glory of the holy name. This is a point, or rather a centre, to which we must return before we are done.

CHAPTER VIII

PHILOSOPHICAL THEODICY

I

THE questions of a teleology or a theodicy of the universe are the final questions and the most fascinating for philosophy, and especially modern philosophy; but they are also the most tantalising. They are just those where philosophy most conspicuously breaks down, whether as an avenue to reality or as a guide of life.

In a great calamity, which goes to the very foundations of the moral soul, and makes us feel as if the bottom had dropped out of the moral world, the poetry which used to delight, uplift, and stay us loses its power; and we turn, as many do at this hour, from poet to prophet, from genius to apostle, from our classics to our New Testament. We turn from imagination to faith, from inspiration to redemption, from all men to Christ, and from all to His Cross. So also we turn from philosophy—not ungrateful, but still unsatisfied. We are slaked rather than fed. It has indeed its vast and ennobling use. In culture poetry itself is hardly so ennobling and so steadying, bringing, perhaps, more elation but less grasp, power, and stay. But philosophy is only the poetry and majesty of thought. It is truth writ very large and impressive to that kind of imagination. And there come crises when from this austere poetry also we turn unfilled and unstayed, and we must go to deeper springs, more eternal powers, and more intimate controls. Truths will not do the work of powers, nor ideals that of faith. From the poetry of great feeling we had to turn, when it was staying power and not refreshment that we needed, to the poetry of great thought—from Byron to Wordsworth, from the empyrean and discursive imagination of Shelley to the penetrative and masculine imagination of Browning. So also, passing on from the spacious poetry of truth in thought, we must turn to the driving power of revelation, from the vast contours of philosophy to the vaster orbits of theology, to the energetic poetry of the Holy and the Eternal. As in the trenches, it is said, some cultured soldiers turn from the love poems that delighted them at home but are adequate no more, to find the soul's mood met only in the Epistles of Paul, so with many more to whom the awful might of evil has been revealed as mid-Europe has revealed it. Face to face with the utmost, the most devilish, forms of suffering and wickedness, they had no stay but in religion's contact with reality, in God's final conquest of both pain and guilt, which Christian faith finds in the Cross of Christ alone as the supreme exercise of the omnipotence of God.

In this ultimate matter of a theodicy philosophy well points out that we have two questions; and before each it is brought to a complete standstill. We have the question of evil as suffering and the question of evil as sin. They are distinct though closely connected. All sin is an ill, but all ill is not sin, nor is it caused by it. Suffering abounded in the animal world before man appeared with the moral freedom that makes sin possible. Pain came before sin, and, as it has no connection with freedom, it is non-moral. And in any theodicy, or justification of God, His treatment of the two is different, to our Christian faith at least. The power in Him can convert suffering to a sacrament, but it must destroy sin. It can transcend and sanctify suffering while the suffering remains, but sin it must abolish. The Cross of Christ can submerge suffering, and make it a means of salvation, but with sin it can make neither use nor terms; it can only make an end of it. God in Christ is capable of suffering and of transmuting sorrow; but of sin He is incapable, and His work is to destroy it. And, by a mystery hard to search, His conversion of the one is the same act as His destruction of the other. His transfiguration of suffering in the Cross is also His conquest of sin. No doubt insoluble problems remain. Why in His creation must the way upward lie through suffering? Why, on this hard hill road, should we be met by sin descending upon us, seized, and flung into the abyss? But at least we can say that it is only one of these, it is the sin not the suffering, that impugns the holiness which makes God God. A holy God might ordain the pain He took on Himself, but he could not ordain the sin. Suffering He could bear directly, but sin only sympathetically. Or though he might sweep away the good and the bad in some great catastrophe of nature, how can He allow the moral perdition even of those who were on the way to goodness, the fall even of the saint?

These questions are quite unanswerable. That is why a book on such a subject is at a disadvantage. We can but fall back on the last choice and committal which we call faith. And that seems to suggest a sermon rather than a discussion. Yet when God came to deal with the position practically and finally it was by the folly of preaching. He took the dogmatic note and not the dialectic. He did not put thought on a new line, but the thinker in a new life. The situation is insolubly irrational, so far as we are concerned. The solution is in action, as Carlyle said,—but in God's, as he did not say. We can but trust God, who by a saving Act masters the thinker and His world, as possessing an answer for thought that He does not yet see fit to give. And above all we must regard Him as having destroyed sin in principle by a way which carries with it also the end of pain. We must regard Him also as destroying evil in practice by methods which seem to us often very devoid and inadequate when we criticise His campaign, but which to Him are perfectly adequate and victorious. We can give God the glory even when He does not increase our joy; for our great object is not the delight of our soul but the glory of God. That sense of sin destroyed He does give us in the experience of our own faith and conscience; but He does not let us pierce with our theoretic reason the deep method and long strategy of His saving Will with the whole world. We may be more sure of our theodicy than clear about our theology. If a science of history be hardly possible, far less possible is a science of God's vindication in history drawn by induction from its course.

Some hard humility becomes our reason here. For its efforts at a solution almost always run out into a slight on conscience. They move the previous question. They pass into a denial of the great crux, either by postulating a limitation on the power of God other than He imposes on Himself (which is to reduce His deity), or by denying the fundamental principle of the conscience, which is the radical and eternal antagonism of good and bad. The philosophic temperament, like the mystic, is too often accompanied by a certain lack of poignant moral sensibility, a certain acquiescence in the morally intolerable, and a lack of the sense of moral tragedy, as of concern for the soul. It is more interested in process than in action, in cohesion than in crisis, in order than in miracle, in growth than in grace. Its tendency is to substitute the æsthetic class of consideration for the moral. It seeks for connection rather than cultivates communion. It does not feel the sting of sin so much as the nuisance of it. It feels it to be an impertinence rather than a revolt. And it is tempted to regard the gulf between the holy and the sinful as more apparent than real, as adjustable in due course by some bridge of device rather than to be closed by a moral crisis and redemption, as something that will yield to evolutionary treatment, to nursing and not operation; as if sin would in due course be abolished like a dangerous blood clot in the general circulation. Sin becomes but a relative stage like everything else, and therefore a relative boon—were it only as something to push against in our ascent. Any notion of an absolute incompatibility and eternal conflict of good and bad is therefore an illusion in this point of view. Progress, culture, will dispel that illusion, and these extreme estimates will vanish, and their antagonisms converge, as they are drawn up into the ascending stream of things. That is to say, ethical values must yield to the mere dynamic movement of a *natura naturans*, quality being submerged in force. This to most will seem the relapse into barbarism. It is always barbarism where moral considerations must be submerged in the natural expansion of a power, a system, or a race, as Germany has shown.

This theory of a development essentially dynamic and not moral is a mere faith in progress now getting out of date. It *is* a faith—but of the inferior and ungrounded kind which easily becomes credulity. This destiny to endless progress cannot be a matter of knowledge; and it may be a superstition, if it has no guarantee beyond a presumption more or less high, and no certainty of a goal. It is at least an illusion, which many cherish, that history must mean advance and not mere movement, and that civilisation carries in it progress as a sort of natural law. Civilisation and progress are identical to so many, that it costs them a great effort to think the two apart. Hence the shock from the war as the outcome of civilisation. We have an almost incurable belief, partly innate, partly inbred, in a Golden Age awaiting society; and it takes much historic thought to discern that the belief in progress was not in antiquity at all, and to realise what an importation it is from Christian faith, and how little there is to sustain it in historic sight. Before Christianity, and outside Israel, the Golden Age was only in the past. When we take a large enough survey, and especially a survey with the ethical eye, the tendency to relapse and degenerate is but little less apparent than the tendency to advance, as Ranke says. And at certain points it gets the upper hand, as it does to-day. The salt and sterile sea rushes up the stream with a huge 'bore.' At any rate, the value before God of each race or stage is not that which can be set forth in terms of civilisation. It is not even to be expressed in terms of culture [1] intellectual and æsthetic. It is something interior to most that is called progress, something which may cause God to think less than we do of our wondrous age, and more than we do of ages that we consider we have long outgrown. A time process like progress cannot be of first moment to the Eternal Spirit who has no after nor before. What is of such moment to Him is timeless acts like grace, redemption, faith, and love. Christ can make good and godly men under any system. Eternity is a much more powerful factor in history than progress. At any rate, the value of an age or people for God (who is an Eternal Simultaneity) is not just what it contributes to other and later stages, but its own response and devotion to Him; and His connection with progress though real is indirect. Progress is much more rapid in the more external and less eternal things; which indicates how little stay it has in itself. Europe has arrived at a crisis in which the expansion of civilisation has rent its crust. Its pace has ruptured its heart. Its collapse reveals the

[1] The historian Lamprecht said that America had civilisation but no culture. By culture he was thinking probably of the mentality produced by a long history and a regard for the past.

spiritual hollowness and the moral perdition within. And the painful process of restoring to progress eternal values is judgment.

It is the practical and moral interests of life that raise these great questions. They did not condense out of the blue sky of abstract themes and speculative dreams. Therefore it is in the region of the soul's moral life that any solution must be found that enables us to go on. It is in the region of faith and in the terms of its theology. The secret of the Lord is not with the philosopher (though God whispers in his ear, it is not that He whispers), but with the prophet.

II

God's justification of us is also His Self-justification. It is in saving our conscience from a doubt of His that He satisfies it and its world problems. That we may have seen. Yet the mind whose peace gives it leisure to think will never cease to find delight and hope in efforts to frame a philosophic theodicy, and to graft the untoward into the general good in some rational way. It has been so from the Stoics to the Illumination, from Leibnitz to De Maistre, and even the Bridgewater Treatises. Philosophy deals but with the ordered course or content of the world under its eyes. It has gradually grown in the power to grasp such law, and to extend its sphere of influence. It is alien to the idea of crisis and tragedy. It cannot therefore admit an absolute contradiction to the world's general success like sin. It is helpless before anything so entirely irrational in kind ; hence its tendency to deny sin as more than the crude instincts unduly prolonged, and its efforts to bring to manageable order the general anomalies of life, and adjust them to its world scheme. It says they are exaggerated, and sets about to reduce the swelling. For this object it has two methods, which we might venture to call those of the buffer and of the shunt. Either it minimises the collision, or it runs the trouble on to a loop line which debouches further ahead into the main line up. It ascribes a good deal to imagination with its habit of exaggerating, or it shows the evil curving round to good and flowing into the general weal. By which I mean more expressly this.

1. The first effort of a philosophic theodicy is to ease the jar, and reduce the impact of the perverse fact on the general mass. The assault on the beneficent scheme of the world is admitted, but it is less than it seems, especially less than it seems to the victims. And it may not be so great as we think even within the consciousness of God, which holds in it but the best of worlds. The Lisbon earthquake, for instance, was explained away by the optimism of the time as no more than a condensation of normal suffering, a precipitation of it at one spot—as on the other side the wide creative processes of growth could be condensed into a miracle like the multiplying of the loaves.

But this is a treatment of evil which, when applied to its worst form, moral evil, is resented by the soul and conscience. The conscience especially has always protested against the comfort got by minimising sin, whose shock to God cannot be reduced without reducing His holiness *pro tanto.* Even our personality has a sense of shock and damage to it from evil too severe and deep to be met by pooh-pooh treatment from the morbidly robust, the ideally vague, the morally dull, or the sentimentally keen—a treatment which comes to a popular head in what is called Christian Science. Pain is not abolished by denying it—except in certain individual cases where the denial superinduces a more or less hypnotic state by auto-suggestion. And the reaction of the personality against such consolations goes so far that it tends to bound into the extreme of pessimism, or a denial of any possible mitigation, any justification, any fundamental teleology. This ends, of course, in the hope for a return to the unconscious chaos from which the world should never have blundered out in the original sin and fall of all. But that pessimism again is resented by the personality on other grounds.

2. So recourse is had to the second method, which is not to soften the collision by a buffer but to avert it by a shunt. The grievance is turned into a loop line, which further on restores it, after some delay, to the main line of harmony. Banes are boons, indirect or inchoate. Grief is but joy misunderstood. Evil is but good in the making. And pain is but friction or detour on a course which is on the whole right. It is a tack to windward. The untoward is only a long and tedious curve into our blessed place in the whole. And the curve itself is still in the whole.

This view is more or less pantheistic, and its monism denies the reality of evil, as dualism denies the Sovereignty of God. Like the other, the 'buffer,' solution, it is resented by the moral personality. It starts with the whole, which is the true good, and where we must resolutely live. It reduces the individual therefore to a resolute subordination. The universal State polices the citizen to his place. The blow or the ache is called but growing pains, or features inevitable in the settling of the atom into this world, where they are but the squeeze at the door. The pain is due to our impatience, our imperfect vision, and our partial treatment of an evolving process. The right sense of the blessed whole would be an anodyne submerging our contributory pain. If we rose to that philosophic height we should 'triumph in a conclusive bliss,' whereas, on the low levels, we 'ache, smallness still, in good that knows no bound.' But this cosmic elevation is not every man's affair, and pain and guilt are. And, in the failure of such a nepenthe, the mind falls again to pessimism from another side, despairs of any teleology or theodicy, and again comes to hope but in a dissolution of reason, and a Nirvana in chaos.

So the philosophic theodicies are apt to break in our hand when applied to the last anomalies of the soul, and to die of their own dialectic. Our faith in God's care for the individual does not arise from our faith in His care for the whole. It is the other way. It is true that His care for me is the source of my faith in His care for the world. I am saved in a saved world. 'O Lamb of God, that takest away the sin of the world, have mercy on *me*.' But it was my salvation that brought home to me how deep it was grounded in the salvation of a world. And I am not saved by my place in the whole, but by my place in Him who redeemed the whole. You may of course speak of a best of all worlds while you deny a providence individual and momentary. But if you do, you are only inverting the error of those who speak of the salvation of a very few, and the consignment of the world at large to neglect or destruction. You are contradicting yourself. If the world of trifles has no providence, and is the region of accident, the world can neither be good nor permanent. There is nothing casual to the good. Trifles flow from eternal laws, and it is Providence in the minute that makes the whole good. The Crucified was amongst the most despised things of earth in that hour; but He has become to the soul that which carries also the burden and future of the whole world.

There is a Christian way of presenting a theodicy of salvation, which is considerably affected by the philosophical method. It tends therefore to be a theosophy rather than a theology, rooted in a thought or idea instead of an act and its experience. And by this leaning it has enjoyed much vogue amongst those who desired to speculate from a Christian and revelationary basis. It did not identify revelation with redemption but treated it as the larger thing, to which redemption was but ancillary. So, starting from this base, it constructed a scheme of the world without reference to sin. It felt, soundly enough, that sin and evil did not possess the right, and therefore had not the power, to thwart for ever God's plan and destiny for mankind. But it tended to underestimate what power they did have, to construe revelation out of relation to them (as if sin affected but a section of the personality), to find it in the process of rational nature or the verdict of the genial soul, and not in the crisis of our last distress and central tragedy, to handle sin in the course of a wider sweep, as the weed goes down under the swath that harvests the corn. It belittled the treatment of guilt to a healing rather than a judgment and a new creation. It was very noble, but it lacked incisive moral realism. It dilated our horizon but it did not search to our marrow. It was in soul too pure, perhaps in blood too poor, to feel the sting of sin, its burning stound and deadly wound. Its conception of the holy was perhaps too celestial and passionless to gauge duly the reaction on sin in the Passion of Christ. It grasped the notion of reconciliation as the nature of God's ideal process in all things, but it did not give its full value to redemption. It did not found reconciliation in the redemption of man or the atonement to God (2 Cor. v. 19 and 21). Its object was to justify God, as it showed by refusing to sin the thwarting power I have named, but it might be said to have failed to glorify God, through its underestimate of sin's malignity and inveteracy which He overcame only in a crisis of Eternity itself. It could not appreciate the passionate tragedy and slavery of man's combined love and hate of sin. It loved in Romans viii., but it had not got there through Romans vii. That is, it made more of the grand and noble than of the holy, and it did not treat sin's antagonism to holiness as killing the life of God in the eye.

It justified God by its effort to picture a world of love and order without sin, and by trusting the healing and recuperative power of this grand moral cosmos in God's hand, its power to reconcile all that marred it, as nature blooms again upon the bloodiest field. This sinless, subduing, reconciling order of the world it saw emerging with commanding power in the history of revelation, and starting there its last stage in the conquest of evil for God's will. But it is doubtful if by its conquest more was really meant than its submersion. The drastic, tragic element of judgment was missing. The critical nature of the conflict was hardly realised in any way adequate to a belief that to destroy sin cost God His life in His Son. The conception of life and of the world was too speculative, too processional, and too little dramatic. Things were not done there. Will and conscience did not come by their own. The world was not God's Act so much as His Movement. Vitality took the place of action, process of crisis, sanity of tragedy. The process of the world was an externalisation of the process in God. It reflected, spread out in time, that balance of movements and tensions which was the eternal stability within the divine nature itself. And it believed that, in due course of this process, the Son would have become incarnate whether sin had entered or not, though in another and happy form, corresponding to the essential divinity of human nature. It worked with natures rather than wills. It was in human nature that sin made most havoc of the divine order. Sin was a flaw there rather than a vice of will. But it could not destroy God's order there; and the divineness of all things was so continued in even fallen man that it must in course submerge and transmute evil as the oyster divinely turns the grit to a pearl. Theology could not therefore in this view be organised from the one centre of grace. Soteriology was not the focus and genius of all revelation. Man is indelibly the summit and compendium of nature as God made it. Therefore a God-man is possible as the very core of that compendium, as the node of the mutual involution of Godhead and finite nature. In Him was crowned, under historic conditions, the process in God which was reflected in creation. The first creation was brought to a head, rather than a new creation begun.

It is of course rather a serious thing to think of the Incarnation as the consummation of a process whether within God, or within the world, or both ; a process whose composure is affected but not fatally perturbed by sin, in which sin is not utterly damning and damnable, only deplorable and dreadful ; a process which moves on to a growing but hardly redemptive reconciliation, of a more or less ideal cast. It all tends to make the agony of the Cross gratuitous, the judgment in it but collateral, the wrath of God a metaphor, and the horror in the guilty conscience overdone. There is something anæmic about the theory, something which leads its sentimentalists to feel 'the blood of Christ' to be now a vulgar phrase. There is a tendency, almost irresistible, away from life's dramatic passion and tragic realism to a pantheistic cheapening of the personality, which is paradoxically concurrent with the equally unchristian deification of Humanity as a whole. It leads to the view of sin which is much in vogue in cultivated religion with an antitheological bias—as something that has on the whole had too much attention, something that is but elemental instinct lingering on in a higher stage, and that is really but a *remora*, or drag, on Humanity, rather than its death and hell. Sin becomes something that, if it cannot be explained away, yet yields to elimination. It is a clot that can become absorbed in the circulation. It does not involve death and rising again in a new creation. And it might, by due skill, even be shown to have been, to the great course of things, a blessing in a deep disguise.

The defect of this view is that it is theosophic and not theological, because it has more philosophy than gospel, and it is less than scriptural. It begins with a wisdom instead of a work, with an impressive theory rather than a saving fact. It gives our knowledge a fresh departure in Christ, but not our world. From the Cross a reconciled world is construed but not created. It starts not from the Cross but from a scheme of the world suffused with Christ and taking the Cross by the way, as if a point might come when it might be forgotten in the larger consummation. It begins with the first creation rather than the second, with spiritual nature rather than Gospel grace; whereas the New Testament works back to the first creation from a foundation in the second; and, if it speak speculatively of a world created in or by Christ, it is with a logic forced by the new and greater creation in Him, the only creation we can experience. It is an inference from the new world realised by experience alone about a region where experience is debarred.

CHAPTER IX

THE ETERNAL CRUCIALITY OF THE CROSS FOR DESTINY

I MADE use in the last lecture of a phrase which I fear may sound to some minds objectionable, not to say offensive; and especially perhaps to those reared in the type of theology which I have just described, with its theosophic theodicy. I spoke of the victory over evil, cosmical or ethical, as costing God His Life. And the phrase certainly brings the issue with that style of theology to a head. Of course there is a sense in which it is nonsense. In the literal sense the death of God would leave the victory with the enemy of God. If God could be abolished there could have been no real God. But the theologian knows that there is a sense in which the phrase is not nonsense, but it gives effect to the absolute antichrist of sin. It expresses that in sin which brings the issue between evil and God to the sharpest issue of the moral world —indeed to the absolute issue of the universe, and which taxes the whole resource of the divine omnipotence in grace. Sin is the death of God. Die sin must or God. Its nature is to go on from indifference to absolute hostility and malignity to the holy; and one must go down. There is no compromise between the holy and the sinful when the issue is seen from the height of heaven to the depth of hell, and followed into the uttermost parts of the soul. And that is the nature of the issue as it is set in the Cross of Christ. It is the eternal holiness in conflict for its life. In the Son of God the whole being of God is staked upon this issue, and His whole campaign with the world; it is not one battle alone; nor is the sin He met but one of many foes. In this conflict the righteousness of God is either secured or lost to the world for ever. It is a question of a final salvation both for man and for God. God there must 'save His word,' which is His Kingdom, which is His Godhead; else the realm of Satan takes its place in control of the world.

Of course when we speak of sin's death and God's there is a certain play upon the word. All sin inflicts a death on God. It is a *diminutio capitis*. It reduces His headship. It imposes on Him a limitation which is quite unlike all His other determinations in that it is not self-determined, and is therefore absolutely intolerable. If His self-determining power were not capable of a determination mightier than the alien one from sin, sin would conquer, and death would reign. But the meaning of the Incarnation is that God was capable, in His self-emptying in Christ, of a self-limitation, *i.e.* a self-mastery of holy surrender, whose moral effect was more than equal to the foreign invasion by sin. He died *unto* sin, as man dies *by* it. But of course death has not the same sense in each case. God carries death as a blessed sacrifice. Sin carries it as an entail of curse. Divine death is moral surrender to sin's conditions but not to its nature. It is an exercise of moral strength and resource which increases life in losing it; whereas the only death at sin's command is decay and destruction. All sin aims at a destruction of God, which His eternal holy life repels; were it unrepelled by the reaction of judgment it would extinguish God. But the reaction and the judgment is that of loving holiness. It is saving judgment. His holiness so dies as to inflict on sin a death which it has not power to repel. There is an experience of death that destroys its deadly power. God's moral (*i.e.* His holy) power converted death itself from the destructive service of sin to His own redeeming service. God in Christ so died that sin lost its chief servant, death, which became now the minister of life, so that its universal curse became universal blessing. Sin, therefore, cost Godhead not Its existence but Its bliss. It cost the Son of God not His soul but all that makes life a conscious fullness and joy. It cost Him the Cross, and all that that meant for such a life as His. God in Christ so met the one enemy as to turn upon him His own weapon of death. God so died as to be the death of death. He commands His own negation—even when it pierces as deep within Himself as His Son. He surmounts the last, the most limiting, phase of finitude—evil. He could so identify Himself with sin and death, His absolute antitheses, that He conquered and abolished both, in an act which brings to a point the constant victory of His moral being.[1] The destiny of the world is whatever does most justice to the nature of God, and most glorifies it. And that is, of all things in the world, the atoning Cross of Christ—where therefore the teleology and the theodicy of the world lies.

Much of our trouble with the theodicy of history has its root, not in a defective view of the connection or causation of events, but in either a poor sense or a false perspective of moral values, even within Christianity itself. May I venture here to expand what I said in the overture to this book? There are plenty, perhaps a majority, of Christian people who would view it as a theological extravagance to be told at the present moment that the greatest, the most tragic, the most portentous occurrence of all man's aching, bloody, and tragic history is the death of Christ; that it is not only the most monstrous but, rising to the region of moral values, it is the most criminal thing that was ever done in the career of Humanity; that it outweighs in gravity and in wickedness all that men or

[1] This line of thought is pursued with fine and deep suggestion in Hegel's *Religionsphilosophie*, ii. 249 ff. Only some caution is required.

nations have done or can do—were even the whole world without exception involved in suicidal war. The eye of God, ranging the ways of men, and reckoning their good and evil as only the Holy can, turns from every crime and every conflict on whatever scale—nay, turns from every other moral achievement in the race, to rest upon the Cross of Christ as the spot where He has set His name for ever, where He has His eternal delight, and where He finds Himself (in the only sense in which Christ's God can) for ever and ever. As He saved man there for Eternity He has also judged man there for Eternity; but also there, bearing Himself the judgment of His own holiness, He has brought in an eternal righteousness by a way which shows Him as not outdone in suffering or sacrifice by any or all of the victims of the whole pain and wickedness of the world. He thus puts Himself into a theodicy which hallows His name for ever as just and good in face of all the sin or evil possible to the most satanic power. But if this be extravagance, it is extravagant only as the relation of an infinite God to a finite world must always be, and as it is the height of extravagance to say at this moment that with God on His throne all is well with the world. Yet He has the evil, even of such a world as we see, in the hollow of His hand. That is the Christian faith. If His holy way spared not His own Son, *i.e.* His own Self, that holiness is secured finally for the whole world, with its most cynical immorality, deadly malignity, and cruel frightfulness. The greatest of all Powers over the world suffered most for it. For Christ went to the Cross as King of the world, and not simply as the kingliest figure in it. He went to the Cross as King, He did not simply come out of it as King. He died as a King, He did not so die that He rose a King. That is the Christian, the apostolic, sense of His historic value. These I say may seem extreme views, couched in extravagant rhetoric which jars upon minds of a different type, training, or experience, minds arrested upon the sanity instead of the tragedy of the world. But then what is a thing like a war that renounces moral and humane controls, but the most extreme shock to our rational culture and ethic? And it is no rationality of the world that can deal with it. Such a historical situation as we now live in need not, perhaps, be accurately stated, if only it is effectively handled. But if it is to be duly stated it cannot be in moderate phrase. Nor can it be handled by moderate rationalisms. It is neither to be met nor mastered but by the extreme resources of God's action with the world, and of our own faith in it. We should have to believe in God even if the war went wrong for us.

But if we do not regard what I have said about the Cross as theological fantasy or preacher's rhetoric, but as apostolic faith calling up its last reserves, then God's Self-justification in history has in view and in control everything history may show to challenge it. We do not here take the quantitative line of striking a balance between the amounts of good and evil in the world, but the qualitative line, the line of values, the line of power at a point —which indeed is the only line on which we can secure the place in the vast universe of that insignificant creature man. In size he is a dwarf, in meaning he is a god. The victory of the holiness of Christ is in command of all the moral phenomena of the world, good or evil. He gained the whole world in gaining His own Soul. If the greatest act in the world, and the greatest crime there, became, by the moral, the holy victory of the Son of God, the source not only of endless blessing to man but of perfect satisfaction and delight to holy God, then there is no crime, not even this war, that is outside His control or impossible for His purpose. There is none that should destroy a faith which is Christian faith indeed, *i.e.* which has its object, source, and sustenance in that Cross and its victory, in which the prince of the world has been in principle judged and doomed for ever. In that Eternal Act (and by no moral process only) the Father's name is hallowed, His Kingdom come, and His will completely met on earth. And we are transported in spirit into the region, not far from any one of us, where these things are always perfectly done and won. It is a solemn and fortifying thought that interior to all space, time, and history there is a world where God's name is perfectly hallowed, His will fully done, and His Kingdom already come. That region is where we retire to renew our moral certainty, behold a royal righteousness, acquire a theodicy more than rational, restore our spiritual strength, and heal our soul's wounds. To have faith unhinged by what we now see is to confess that it was a faith unfounded and unfed from the eternal source. It is to own that our faith arose elsewhere than at Christ's Cross. No wonder therefore that a twilight comes on our God. We have missed His tryst in His Son, and we think, as the gloom deepens, that He is late. But it is a new mercy of God (as His judgment always is) that lets the false foundation slide from us, so that we may stand, in its debacle, on the Rock that nothing can shake. 'But this is escaping into religion.' Surely. Is there any other escape from the world's worst ? 'But it means the foundation of morals in theology.' No doubt. There is no help for it. There is no final ethic but a theological. When your happy world goes to pieces, you cannot believe in a moral world except in the faith of such a revelation as took effect in the moral redemption of the universal conscience, and which secured for ever the holiness of God out of the worst that man can do.

With the collapse now of a religion chiefly humanitarian there goes also the 'this-worldliness' which has been such a bondage and a blight upon religion. When we are startled out of our satisfaction with enlightened man and an exploited God by the Superman's super-moral attempt to come to his own in this world, we are driven into a new belief in another world, in Immortality. We are driven to find more meaning, and perhaps spend more time, in God's realm of eternal lordship by love, His righteousness perfectly holy, and His universal grace. It would be impossible to believe in His love or His Kingdom if we could not call in another world to redress the balance of this, or rather to answer its groaning prayer. Science explains its universe by going back to the action of infinite power for millions of years; but faith explains its world by going forward to God's action in eternity. And this it can only do with certainty by going down as deep as Eternity is long—down into His action in Jesus Christ. There is but one point in time where the length and the breadth and the depth of the Eternal City are equal: it is the spot where, on the Cross, the holy Son of God is slain from before the foundation of the world for its eternal redemption. And, just as history shows, in the long reach of time now open to it, changes which, passing from material to moral, are qualitative in values and not only quantitative in structure, so faith, in the contemplation of eternity, recognises a like change into the highest kind. The sacrificial death, say, in battle, even of those who are not in Christ, must surely mean much for their approach to Him, and for the opening of their eyes to a blessing that begins with fear. And the dead in Christ see a more wondrous Christ than we do—the same, indeed, yesterday, to-day and for ever, yet another. There is a new departure for them in Christ's work, which is greater than when their eyes were opened to Him here, even as the second creation is greater than the first. Christ's contact with the dead is a new and greater phase of the new creation. It makes, for the history of the race continued into the unseen, an epoch parallel to that created by His entrance upon flesh which made our access to Him at the first.

And with the new order of life comes a new vision of values, not less revolutionary, perhaps, than when He changed our life in our own earthly days. We may expect there a judgment of all past things which is as revolutionary to our present standards as our conscience would seem to the wild boar from the woods which imperially devours the more helpless denizens of the earth. More people may be converted beyond by the experience of death than here by fear of it. There is much mischievous nonsense talked, and many irreverent pictures drawn, about the welcome by Christ of the soldier, whatever his manner of life, who left all and followed the call of country to death on the field. It was a fine thing to do, but let us not spoil it by extravagance of this kind. There is no true sacrifice for righteousness but has its reward. And the chief reward for such an act may be the gift of saving shame and repentance for the life it closed. The patriotic sacrifice may have lifted the soul to the level where the steep slopes to Christ's Cross really began.

To our present conscience there is no solution of the awful doings whereof we are compelled to be a part. Yet it is we who are at a loss, it is not God. We have no vision of a moral harmony that submerges misery and evil, and spreads to order all, but we trust One who has not vision only but command; and we have absolute ground for trusting Him in Jesus Christ the Agent, and not but the seer, of the world reconciliation. Not only can God solve the world, He has solved it, in His own practical way of solution, by saving it—by an act done, and not a proof led, nor a scheme shown. His wisdom none can trace, and His ways are past finding out; but His work finds us; and His grace, His victory, and His goal become sure. If we saw all His scheme our faith would be compelled, and not free. It might do more to overwhelm us than to raise or fortify. It would be sight—something too satisfactory to a merely distributive justice;

it would not be faith creative and constitutive for the holy soul. The faith we keep means more for our soul than the views we win. Job's friends had sounder views on some points than he, but they did not receive the reward that his desperate faith had. In the Cross of Christ we learn the faith that things not willed by God are yet worked up by God. In a divine irony, man's greatest crime turns God's greatest boon. *O felix culpa!* The riddle is insoluble but the fact is sure. The new man, remade in Christ and not simply impressed by Christ, is sure amid a world of strident problems. We know what God has done for the world in redeeming it; we have tasted that in our soul; but we do not know why He took the way with it that He did, why it must mean the Cross. He speaks not an all-solving but an all-liberating word. Again, no theodicy is possible, and no peace, except to an evangelical faith.

That is to say, the only teleology is miraculous. It is not catastrophic like the early eschatologies, but it keeps the element in them which catastrophe covered—the element of crisis and miracle. And above all, it keeps the element which miracle covered, the element of grace—the miracle of miracles. It is a matter of grace. Nature is not sure enough of itself to promise its own consummation. Evolution is not *per se* redemptive. This is especially borne in on us when we have to do with a moral teleology, with a theodicy. It is hard to realise the moral destiny in nature, its deep travail with the Kingdom of God's love. It is still harder to find this in the range next above nature—in human freedom, in man's treatment of man, where we have not simply inadequacy but perversity. And hardest of all is it to see it in man's treatment of the saint, the man of grace. Yet it is here that the worst turns the best for our faith, and redeems all beside. It is the persecuted saint that least doubts and most trusts the goodness of God. It was one who felt himself treated by the world as among the off-scouring of all things who was sure that all things worked together for good to them that love God for His purpose. Out of the abuse and wreck of natural freedom rises the supernatural liberty of the sons of God, with its vindication of God in its justification of man. The grand purpose and justification of all that went before is the righteousness of God secured by the miraculous grace of the Cross, its hallowing of God's name in all nature and history, and its suborning of all evil to the service, increase, and praise of eternal good. The miracle of grace is the rescue of a world where rational order failed to secure its own end, yet found its own soul. So it is the final theodicy of the world. The world was made for grace, made in the first creation by One who had in reserve all the resources of the second. Man was made at first to be redeemed at last. Is this reality or rhetoric—moral reality or religious fancy ? Does God's holy love come to its own only in His miracle of grace ? In atoning grace does love give law a place of honour that law failed to secure for itself ? It is the miracle of grace that glorifies the law it seems to break, by destroying the sin that really broke it. The miracle of the Cross broke no law, but it healed and honoured the law that sin broke. The greatest law in all things is their deep and subtle convergence on such miracle. All process serves personality and its mysterious freedom, and above all its freedom in grace. The miracle of the Kingdom, the conversion of the will, is the 'truth' of all law, its inmost content and eternal burthen. Law is great with miracle. It comes to itself in it, blossoms in it. What heals its wound reveals its nature as God's servant, magnifies it, honours it, and pacifies all the wounds it received. No glozing by optimism of the hateful facts does what is done by their redemption in Christ. Sin is so sinful to none as to the Saviour from it. To mitigate the moral situation is useless. We are shut up thoroughly—to mercy.

The only theodicy is that which redeems, and from the nettle perdition plucks the flower of salvation. But it should be very clear that redemption is not a theodicy except by the way of an atonement which does justice to God's holiness and the righteousness in things. Salvation is a theodicy only by the way of a justification which places man in the position not of God's beneficiary only but of God's son in Christ. And such is the fullness of the redemption of the Cross. It does not simply place us in a warm fellowship, and move us to the adoration of Him who loved us and gave Himself for us; but it also places us in a holy Kingdom, and lifts us out of devout groups to the righteousness which exalts nations in their very blood, and the holiness of God whose indwelling makes a Church.

I have said much about the certainty that we have of the great goal of the world, on the security of what God, with His eyes open to everything, has done for it once for all in Christ. I have said that this goal so secured is not simply the end that all history makes for in the future, but also the most present, deep, and potent ground within every stage of its movement thereto. That is the work of the Spirit—to make us realise the Simultaneity of Eternity in time. If we look back, faith, by the Spirit, abolishes time, and finds the fontal Christ of long ago to be the fundamental power of to-day. He rose upon history in a remote age, and He rises in history now from its profoundest depths. So, looking forward, the same faith, by the same Spirit, realises His final goal of the Kingdom to be the deepest of all forces in history—retroacting, shall we say, however indirectly, in every age. The soul's future goal is its present ground. Of all the Great Powers the greatest is the purpose of God, which we are to love. The Kingdom of God is the most tremendous power active among us at this moment, though it is conspicuously working for the time in its negative function of judgment. But it is always judgment unto positive salvation. It is the saving power that judges. It is this God, I have said, this Identity of yesterday, to-day, and for ever in Christ and His redemption, that gives us any faith in a teleology, and therefore (since He is holy) in a theodicy in things. No rational theodicy or philosophic certainty is possible with our knowledge. But faith is not a poor second best, nor an easy exit. It is no small nor light victory of faith to have found our footing in such an end, and to be sure that good will be the final goal of ill. But, even when we are secure there, it is hardly a less conflict and a less victory to keep sure—to keep sure that this is the immanent and informing principle which is working its way to the surface in history, whether by process or convulsion. We have been tempted to think that, while the goal is sure, it might perhaps be reached by the destruction of the world, and the salvation of a very few in some ark to re-stock the new æon. It costs faith much, when it has become sure of the goal, to be sure also that that goal is always within us as the greatest of all the Great Powers that shape the great politics of history; that it is not regulative only for the trend of history but constitutive for its genius; that, suffusing all, there is a grand 'stratagem of moral reason' which exploits the very folly and crime of war, and which we call by a better name as 'the manifold wisdom of God.' It is not easy to believe that the Kingdom of God is the greatest Empire now in the world—and especially at present is it hard. But faith's greatest conquest of the world is to believe, on the strength of Christ's Cross, that the world has been overcome, and that the nations which rage so furiously are still in the leash of the redeeming God.

I came a little ago to allude to the value, for the purpose of a theodicy, of the reality of a future life. I would now point out its bearing on our view of God's *modus operandi*.

There are two things that faith must bear in mind here: first, that God's method is revealed as one of election; second, that it is one of sorrow. The Captain of the elect was not spared the Cross. 'Christ is crucified to the world's end,' as Pascal says.

1. God's method, His way to His goal, is that of an election, in which He is absolutely free. Any theodicy must be much affected when we cease to prescribe a rational programme for the Almighty Wisdom, and leave Him who has the end already secure to choose freely the fitting way to it. It is so easy to set up an expectation and call on God to comply. It is so easy to frame some high *priori* way, and pitch our demand accordingly, as to what God would do. It is not so easy to ask what God has done, penetrate it, and accept His own account of His way of doing it. I would here return to a note I struck at the outset, and put it as pointedly as I can.

In the quest for a theodicy what is it that you are looking for? What is it that would justify God to you? You have grown up in an age that has not yet got over the delight of having discovered in evolution the key to creation. You saw the long expanding series broadening to the perfect day. You saw it foreshortened in the long perspective, peak rising on peak, each successively catching the ascending sun. The dark valleys, antres vast, and deserts horrible, you did not see. They were crumpled in the tract of time, and folded away from sight. The roaring rivers and thunders, the convulsions and voices, the awful conflicts latent in nature's ascent and man's—you could pass these over in the sweep of your glance. They were subterranean to your calm purview. You never lived through one of these cosmic wars. So you easily framed to yourself a long panorama of rising evolution, and that steady crescendo became your standard of expectation. You pictured the world and the race unfolding their powers, achievements, and joys in a waxing process of beneficent triumph, spreading light, and broadening boon. But now you have been flung into one of these awful valleys. You taste what it has cost, thousands of times over, to pass from range to range of those illuminated heights. You are in bloody, monstrous, and deadly dark. You taste an unspeakable misery, which may well make you question if any progress is worth its cost—especially the progress that cannot forfend such misery. Every æsthetic view of the world is blotted out by human wickedness and suffering. The air is red as the rains of hell. The rocks you stood on fall on you. With the expectations you framed from your old æsthetic survey you bring to book the Power deep within it all. You complain that God has deceived you and you were deceived. You see no sense, no justice in it. No general blessing, even when peace returns, can atone for this. And so on. God has not kept His promise. Or He has been unable to pursue His way.

His promise! What was it? Your expectation? What right had you to take your expectation for promise? Where did you frame it? His way? Where did you discover that? Evolution? Is that His last word? Does evolution itself not go on by incessant selection and survival from horrors? Have you been putting all the stress on the evolution and none on the selection, all on the evolutionary process and not the selective action? Have you been watching the career of the cosmos, and ignoring the way of the conscience? Is it there, in the world's long process, and not in the great providential personalities and junctures, that God has been saying His great Word and opening His deep mind? Have you searched history and its moral crises as you should? If you have, have you only been looking at the nineteenth century? Have you taken due notice of the first? There is a history within history that comes to a point there. There is, within evolution, a history of redemption, where selection rises to election, and, ceasing to be the play of powers, becomes a Person's Act. Have you framed your expectations on social evolution alone, with no regard to divine election ? Have you hoped for everything by the way of broadening permeation, and not at all by the way of sifting judgment, all by growth and none by dilemma ? Has the strait gate been removed from the broad road ? Is it all procession and no agonising ? Have you been at close quarters with the movement, the actions, of your own soul ? Have you touched the nerve of *its* history ? Have you really been through Romans vii. ? Or is it but the æsthetic splendour of Romans viii., its academic, its imaginative depth, that has held you ? Have you been brought, pastorally or otherwise, in contact with but one of those cases that represent the moral condition of the race, where one vice has poisoned, and, in the end, paralysed the whole personality, and, slowly mouldering, surely ruined all ? Do you know moral tragedy, or only moral pathology ?

Will you not have to question anew the real source of moral hope, and revise your expectation there ? You may have to give up the idea of a spreading and beautiful Humanity as the paradigm of history. It is not growing like a tree in bulk that makes man better. That is but a process, and no mere process does justice to human freedom and moral worth. The soul goes through much more than a process. You may have—and this dire experience is what is to make you—you may have to take to the more slow and complex idea of an elect. If you take account of your Bible, the text-book of the world's redemption, it is what you will find there. Salvation and election are not separable there—a goal of universal salvation, worked out by a method of particular election. You will have to recast your ideas of progress to meet the case of moral growth. That does not come by gradual expansion, illumination, and amelioration, but more by crisis, choice, judgment, sifting, election, conversion, and new departure by new creation age after age—yea, long into eternity (for, as it is a supernatural process, it has not nature's limit of death). One elect succeeds another, and each lives for all in rising cycles. From the non-elect in one stage comes the elect for the next. And so on, in an ascending series of elects, till the whole human lump is refined, till all are brought in—the worst and most intractable last, since freedom may not be forced. There is all eternity to do it in. Here time is no longer. The ungathered fruit of one age yields seed for the next. What seems the wreck of one civilisation is but the shaling of the next. What seem to us waste products they have means of using and refining behind the veil. And so the elective process goes on—the elite serving the submerged in every cycle—till we all come to the fullness and quality of the universal and eternal Christ.

The same fallacy of expectation takes another shape. We not only formed our hopes on an order of evolution instead of a crisis of revelation, of revolution, and redemption, but we caught ourselves cherishing, subconsciously, and as a matter of course, the notion that the ends of history had come upon us. We thought like this. If not quite at the end this age is within sight of it. We have now for a long time had our bearings right and our final course set. The grand social paradise has begun, in the sense that we all feel the imperative of it. We have got the principle of it and it has but to be worked out on the lines of the most enlightened publicists, philanthropists, and moralists. The closing cycle rich in God has come. We are now near the top of the toilsome slope, and close on the plateau on which the city of God begins to rise.

The triumphs of civilisation have brought along the wondrous age. There have been none like it, scientifically or socially. We are on the edge of a new dispensation—of progress indeed, but of progress on the level, of expansion, dilation, enrichment. We have reached a relative finality, and we have but to consolidate and exploit the ideas and conquests that development has won for good and all. The glories of civilisation represent the consummation of God's beneficent plan; they need but to be popularised. So we thought. That is the frame of mind we have been living in, and we have been treating as a postulate of all further expectation.

It has been rudely shaken. We are not where we thought. Satan is loose for a season. We are not at the end of the climbing. A worse range faces us. If we were at the end of a stage it was but on one line of advance. Civilisation has but thrust one long salient into barbarism, and it is beaten back. We were going suspiciously fast and easy. Because it was a progress too dashing. We did not carry with us our supplies or our moral reserves. We took the ridge, but our supports did not come up, and we have to retire with great loss. We have fallen into an ambush. Our light cavalry have been pulled upon their haunches at an abyss, and many have gone over. The rest have to retire and pick up our moral civilisation, left much behind by our headlong material advance. And this arrest of evolution, this shock of recovery, disaster though it be, is in the way of judgment,—so indispensable to the divine theodicy. If it is a collapse, it is still more the assertion of the moral world and its conditions, the irruption of the Kingdom of God. We had not reached even a relative finality. Finality does not come on that line. In civilisation there is no rest. It has no Sabbath. It would even abolish Sunday. Anything like finality is gauged not by mere advance, but by our contact maintained with the whole and its goal.

It is only our possession of the goal that gives us any means of estimating the stage, or even calling it a stage, and not an excursion or a freak. But that whole, that goal, is in another world. It is too great for earth. There is not room enough in this world for God's eschatology. In another world alone we rest from our vertical ascent, so to say, with its labour and sorrow, and we extend laterally. We expatiate on God's plane. We develop inwardly. We cease to be the mere nomads of progress, and we set to acquire spiritual wealth, and to build the city of God on His shining tableland. But is that not other-worldliness? No; for that other world is not future merely, but eternal. Eternity is the only safe measure of progress; and to live there is our only security in it. The whole of God's plan embraces past, present, and future. It pervades our history, though in another world only does it 'arrive.' It is in history but not of it. It emerges in history, but from heaven not from earth. There is a point in the past where it is condensed and creative for eternity, where, as in man's personality, we have eternity in a point. It is in Christ, and in the crucial action of Christ on His Cross, which overcame the world, and created the new heaven and the new earth.

We create difficulties for ourselves, I say, by our wrong start, by expectation formed at other sources than God's own account of His profound and supreme way. We go to nature and we forget human freedom; to evolution and we neglect election; to history and we leave out the Bible; to the heart and we succumb to subjectivism and ignore Christ; to love and we omit its preferential and selective way. And hence these troubles and these tears.

2. But, second, the method of election might be granted, on the large lines of eternal process that I have drawn, and yet the question remains as to suffering. Why such dreadful and ineffable suffering along the whole course, suffering both of those taken and those left? Why does

it cost so much at every stage to elicit the elect? And why does it cost not only to the elect but to those who do not seem elect, and do not inherit the far-off interest of their tears?

To that question less even than to the former is there any rational answer, except in so far as real faith is implicitly rational. There is an Eye, a Mind, a Heart, before Whom the whole bloody and tortured stream of evolutionary growth has flowed. We are horrified, beyond word or conception, by the agony and devilry of war, but, after all, it only discharges upon us, as it were from a nozzle, a far vaster accumulation of such things, permeating the total career of history since ever a sensitive organism and a heartless egoism appeared. This misery of the ages, I have said, vanishes from human thought or feeling, till some experience like the present carries some idea of it home. But there is a consciousness to which it is all and always present. And in the full view of it He has spoken. As it might be thus: 'Do you stumble at the cost? It has cost Me more than you—Me who see and feel it all more than you who feel it but as atoms might. "Groanings all and moanings, none of it I lose." Yea, it has cost Me more than if the price paid were all Mankind. For it cost Me My only and beloved Son to justify My name of righteousness, and to realise the destiny of My creature in holy love. And all mankind is not so great and dear as He. Nor is its suffering the enormity in a moral world that His Cross is. I am no spectator of the course of things, and no speculator on the result. I spared not My own Son. We carried the load that crushes you. It bowed Him into the ground. On the third day He rose with a new creation in His hand, and a regenerate world, and all things working together for good to love and the holy purpose in love. And what He did I did. How I did it? How I do it? This you know not now, and could not, but you shall know hereafter. There are things the Father must keep in His own hand. Be still and know that I am God, whose mercy is as His majesty, and His omnipotence is chiefly in forgiving, and redeeming, and settling all souls in worship in the temple of a new heaven and earth full of holiness. In that day the anguish will be forgotten for joy that a New Humanity is born into the world.'

But all this is groundless if in the Cross of Christ we have but the love of God shown in sacrifice and not its holiness secured in judgment; if the Cross be but to reconcile man and not atone to God, to impress many and not first to hallow the holy name.

I take up here a word to make it clear that the confidence of soul which is called for by the great convulsions of history is something more than an intense but vague reliance on the love of God, even as that is manifested in Christ. We need more than a general trust of His heavenly kindness. The Christian teleology of a world like this demands more than a conviction of the overflowing goodness of God's will towards us, submerging the wrath of man. That God is love is a very great faith, to be sure, as things are. But we need more. Has this love all power in heaven and on earth? Is it final? Is it eternal? Can I be sure that He has power to give His love final and eternal effect? At the very last pinch is His love, perhaps, helpless against the loveless power? Is the last victory in any degree doubtful? The faith which overcomes such a world—is it just to be sure of the love of God towards it, while we have no means of certainty that this love is identical with the last reality and sovereign power of all things for ever? Is the Cross of Christ but the manifestation of a love that would certainly be the blessing and joy of the universe if it could only establish itself in it and over it for eternity? Must we not go further than that with our faith in the Cross and the Son of God, further even than a faith in Christ as the Eternal Son? Is He Eternal King? He is such *de jure*, will He at last be such *de facto*? Is the power equal to the love? Is the King as universal as the Father? Is the Kingship and its judgment a constituent element of the Father? The soul in history, in its experience of the world, is distracted between the spectacles of loveless power and powerless love. Power is cruel, kindness is feeble. This is the observation that at a great crisis wrecks the faith of so many of the finer kind who can rest content with neither. It is the antinomy in life that most needs adjustment and solution if we are to believe that God is love and power is grace, and omnipotence redemption. And it is that solution or nothing that Christ brings. If He do not bring it, He but accentuates the intolerable situation. Love then seems more helpless than ever, going under to power; power more heartless than ever crushing love. Must we not go on to find and trust in the Cross something more absolute even than universal, something which does not simply promise the final victory, but achieves it, something which is the crucial act of the world's King, and not simply an act which ought to make Him that King, if right had might. Has He not only value for us but right, nor only right but equal might? Is the last enemy already destroyed in the Cross? Is the last victory won? Are all things already put under the feet of God's love and grace? Have we in the Cross of Christ the crisis of all spiritual existence? The Christian religion stands or falls with the answer of Yes to such questions. In His Cross, Resurrection and Pentecost, Christ is the Son of God's love *with power*. God's love is the principle and *power* of all being. It is established in Christ everywhere and for ever. Love so universal is also absolute and final. The world is His, whether in maelstrom or volcano, whether it sink to Beelzebub's grossness or rise to Lucifer's pride and culture. The thing is done, it is not to do. 'Be of good cheer, I *have* overcome the world.' 'This is the victory which *has* overcome the world—your faith.' The only teleology is a theodicy, and the only theodicy is theological and evangelical.

If it is needful that the moral idea become still more pointed, we must put it that the only possible theodicy is an adequate atonement. A mere vast and impressive exhibition of God's love is not enough. The element in divine love which makes its mastery and eternity is the holiness of it. This is its eternal rock and power if the real is the moral and if morality is the nature of things. What must be secured for the sake of love's true deity and last control is its holiness? But holiness is not anything that can just be shown; it must be done. Here revelation is action. Not only must God's love be poured out on His world but, as holy love, it must be established in command of it. The holiness of love's judgment must be freely, lovingly, and practically confessed from the side of the culprit world. It must be answered with perfect holiness, *i.e.* with the Supreme Act of God and man in history, the Supreme Act of the world's King and conscience. This wedding of man's conscience and God's is the great and final theodicy. And that took place in the atoning Cross.

What do we really want when we ask for a theodicy? Is it not the adjustment in principle of the state of the world and the character of God? But the character of God we know only by His supreme revelation of Himself; it is by no inference or presumption of ours, by no transfer of our instincts and impressions to Him. It comes, therefore, from the objective revelation historic in Christ; and chiefly, where that came to a head, in Christ's Cross. And as to the state of the world, that means at last the moral state of man. The wrongest thing with the world is its sin. War, being wicked, is a worse anomaly than pestilence or famine. If a theodicy, then, is called for it is because either God seems to fail a deserving world and does not treat it justly, or a perverse world fails a righteous God and does not treat Him justly. Now any real Theism, and especially the Christian faith in the Cross, is bound up with the absolute holiness of God, and it cannot therefore start with a human ideal which God is thought to betray when we bring Him to its bar. We must begin with a righteous God revealed, whom the world fails, renounces, and defies. This is the religious view of the world. The other is not religious; it may be rational or philosophical; and between religion and philosophy it is not a matter of argument and its compulsions but of choice and its freedom.

But if it is a case of a defective world and a perfect God in collision, a sinful world and a holy God, then the right relation between them, the only relation that does justice to the rightness of God, is the world's attitude of repentance before the Holy and trust in His grace. The only rightness of a world awry is the confession of wrongness. But the further the world is out of tune with such a God the less able is it to realise its wrongness and to repent, the less adequate is any such repentance as it has, and the less sure can it be that the holy which condemns it is also to be trusted as grace. How can a sinful world adequately confess in practice a holiness to which its sin makes it ever weaker and blinder? How can it do justice to it? How justify God, or realise what would be His right treatment of the world? How can it do honour to a holiness which can be honoured and justified by holiness alone? How can it answer with its soul and conduct the righteousness of God's? How can God secure His righteousness in the face of such a world? He can neither undo its evil past, nor ensure its better future. That is what we want in a real and searching theodicy—the righteousness of God not only admitted but adored, not only dreamed but done—and done in a world not of suffering alone but still more of sin. Can God so secure His righteousness that the unrighteous world shall be His praise? Can He get such a world to call Him, from the heart of its evil, guilt, and misery, and under the ban of His judgment, yet holy, wise, and good? That would be the supreme theodicy, the last justification of God, uttered in silent action by a Humanity that forgets its own fate in entire concern for His righteousness and glory.

But that is what we have in Christ's atoning Cross. There we have the one perfect, silent, and practical confession of God's righteousness, which is the one rightness for what we have come to be, the one right attitude of the world's conscience to God's. In Him Humanity justifies God and praises Him in its nadir; and that is the great theodicy. But if that Christ crucified do justice to the holiness of God, confessing it, while under its judgment, with a holiness equal to the Father's own, and offering amid suffering an obedience perfect as mere suffering can never be—then we have the atonement; which is not just suffering for us, for suffering, being non-moral in itself, cannot be perfect or holy or satisfying to God. We have then the perfect satisfaction the Holy finds in the Holy, and the delight of the Father in a Son with whom He is always well pleased. That holiness of the Son of God is the complete reparation to the holiness of God the Father. But if it is made by the Son of God it is made by God. God could be atoned by no outside party. And the Father suffered in His Son even more than the Son did. Further, if Christ was the Son of man the reparation was made by man in Him. Christ was the new Humanity doing the one needful and right thing before God. God's justification of man, therefore, was by His justification of Himself in man. The last theodicy is a gift of God and not man's discovery nor an achievement. It is not a rational triumph but the victory of faith. Christ is the theodicy of God and the justifier both of God and the ungodly. The supreme theodicy is atonement.

CHAPTER X

SAVING JUDGMENT

I HAVE so often alluded to the tragedy of history as being for Christian faith the judgment of God, and therefore His salvation, that I wish to speak of it more than allusively, as God's saving way with the world. The more we believe in the Kingdom of God the more we must believe in judgment.

The great Christian message to the world is not simply love. That is too general, not to say vague. Christianity does not produce only love to God, but also hate. It not only produces faith but it also deepens unfaith, and hardens impenitence. If it loose it also binds; and it can do the one only if it do the other—action and reaction being equal. If it draw some near to God, it repels others into distance and estrangement. There is such a thing as the repulsive power of a great affection. To say that the revelation is only love is not relevant enough to the actual and moral situation of a world which is something else than love-hungry. Nor does it do justice to the New Testament, with its ruling note of the holy, and its supreme gift of a Holy Ghost. The message is to the conscience, and it is moral reconciliation. Such is the prime and positive revelation—the holy God in Christ reconciling the sinful world to Himself. That is to say, the Christian Gospel is not simply to exhibit God's love. His love might be a helpless passion if he had not an equal power behind it. But that power Christ exerts. His

Gospel secures not love's exhibition but its final domination of all things and all foes. It does not show something; it does something. And in that action judgment is essential. The victory of grace in the Kingship of God involves certain factors subordinate, and, in a sense, negative, though vital; and if reconciliation is the obverse of the Cross, judgment is its reverse. Grace and judgment were both revealed, and both exercised, in the same act of Christ. Perfect grace was and is final judgment. It is condemnation to ignore salvation. Full and final judgment is not something superadded to the Gospel. It is no corollary, no by-product. It is intrinsic to it. It is an element of Fatherhood, and not a device.[1] It is an effect of the preaching of the Gospel which is organic with the salvation in it. The same Church that evangelises the world in the very act judges it. It not only divides each soul, but all society, electing and rejecting. The classic passage on the reconciliation (2 Cor. v. 19) is followed, immediately and epexegetically, by the moral theme of expiation or judgment (v. 21), without which the New Testament does not regard reconciliation as possible. So that, while the ruling note of Christian preaching must always be reconciliation, judgment is there as a subdominant, giving the reconciliation its quality as moral. The Cross did not, indeed, come directly and expressly to judge (John viii. 15-16, xii. 47–48). It did so only in the course of exerting (I wish to say more than revealing) God's love, grace, and forgiveness. But judge it certainly did. It brought to a head for the world the sin of an elect nation—a nation whose sense of privilege and merit repudiated moral for national interests, scouted Christ's word of mercy and His call to

[1] The Grotian theory of Christ's Cross as a penal example or object-lesson, and not a reaction of judgment intrinsic to God's holiness, is a case of substituting a device of God for an element in Him. Judgment is an essential element in Fatherhood. and not a corrective device.

repent, and found no public meaning in His Word of love and humility. It thus became, more than Rome, incarnate Antichrist. It sinned against pure light. The Cross which that nation inflicted filled up the measure of its guilt and brought it death. And this was not against Christ's will but with it. He knew He was Israel's doom. The Holy One knew that the soul of man or nation that chose to sin must go on to die, and that every word of greater love might become a word of more wrath. But He never judged them in the sense of avenging, far less of revenging. Their judgment was the reaction on them, from God's holiness, of their fatal misconception of holiness, the recoil of their egoist and self-satisfied righteousness, of their own deed in rejecting a holy reconciliation as needless, and reckoning rather on reward. It was the irony of a holy God on the sanctity of wrong-headed and self-sure worshippers, worshippers full of sacrifice but of saltless sacrifice, indiscriminate sacrifice, sacrifice as a passion only, full of ideal rage but void of faith with its moral insight and its sound judgment. It was the nemesis on their Semitic hate. It is valuable at this juncture, when the bearing of moral principle on national conduct is denied even by German religion, to remember that the greatest sin the world committed was a national and religious sin, culminating in national hate, and then in national destruction. But the heart of Christ is not irony, whatever use He made of irony. And though Providence is ironical it is not irony. The heart of all is mercy. That is the supreme function of the Cross. It is the action, the omnipotence, of grace. Sacrifice is good or bad as it serves or hinders that moral end. Christ bore evil, He did not avenge it. He so bore it as to judge and destroy it, which mere nemesis, mere punishment, cannot do; and because it cannot, it is less true than judgment. Christ certainly used force, and gave it His moral sanction. He racked the victim of the unclean spirits in exorcising them. He cowed His disciples, He did not only impress them. He preached hell as in the service of His kingdom. He "hewed" the Pharisees. And His prediction of Jerusalem's ruin in war with Rome was (from Him) more than a prediction, it was an infliction. War as judgment is the servant of righteousness, and righteousness is the twin of grace. Crisis means, behind it all and in proportion to its greatness, the kingdom of God and a new creation. The phrase 'progress by crisis' is the modern variant of the old 'salvation by judgment.' We seek first the positive kingdom, and therewith such negative judgment as it requires.

There may even be times when the idea of judgment is the more urgent side of the kingdom. There are junctures when the interest of the grand reconciliation requires that the attention of the world should be recalled with iterant stress to the principle of judgment, however contributory its place may be in the whole relation. Of such junctures the present situation may be one. And for several reasons. First, a sweet and cheery type of religion has come to prevail which prospers well, with its winsome Christ and its wooing note, but which (whether we call it sentimental, æsthetical, or optimist) has all but banished the idea of judgment from the Christian ethics, just as it deprecates the notion of atonement in its pious type. This not only departs from the New Testament idea but it is laden with the gravest moral weakness. It must be so, if religion at every point is holy, if the power of the Gospel is the righteousness of God (Rom. i. 17), if its atoning redemption of the conscience has a vital effect on morality, if the faith of the Cross is the source of Christian ethic, and at last of all ethic. Second, the idea of the kingdom has in the last half-century had more attention than result; which is due in part to the moral defect involved in its detachment from this idea of righteousness in the Cross of Christ. And, third, the awful events amid which we live can by no Christian mind be treated merely as a crunch of progress, as the grinding of the historical glacier turning a corner in its onward course. Nor are they merely a poisonous by-product of civilisation. They are an assertion of the moral order which, after all, controls civilisation, so that what it has sowed it now reaps. They make an apocalypse, which the moral levity of our very religion much needed, of the awful nature of evil. They are, like Israel's part in the death of Christ, a revelation of Satan vying with that of God. So the wrath of God leaps out upon the unrighteousness of men. East or West, the nations shall be cast into hell that forget a holy God. These events form a negative and purgative element in the coming of God's kingdom of reconciliation. They are to be integrated into its aspect of atonement, expiation, the solemn and blessed bearing of judgment. They are the rear view of the Cross of Christ and its historic salvation. And they offer us, indeed they force on us, an occasion to amend, by fresh attention, much neglect of the Cross as the final principle and moral measure of all history. They set us on so to trace the immanence of its action in man's whole career that we can believe in a divine judgment in history in spite of history. If God spared not His own Son He can bear to see, and rise to use, the most dreadful things that civilisation can produce. History is a long judgment process; but it is not in the course of history with its debacles that we find the last judgment of God, and fix our faith in it, but at a point of history, in the Cross of Christ. It is there that we find the justification of God at first hand, and His own theodicy.

Judgment by God is in the Bible a function of His action as King. And to this day, when the due sense of God's kingship goes, the sense of judgment goes with it; and the type of religion, however winsome, sinks accordingly in one kind to moral pusillanimity, and in another to racial ferocity, as we see these in the German Church on the one hand and the German State on the other. With the loss from the heart of our religion of the note of judgment goes the sense of public righteousness and national responsibility; and therefrom come in the end public meanness, madness, infatuation, and collapse. A faith in mere fatherhood will not carry a nation's conscience; it will not save it from national egoism; nor will it serve the more public ends of religion, however it may sweeten its private note. And it is the public and social failure of religion that is our chief trouble at this hour, either at home or abroad.

I would say much in little in venturing the opinion that the favourite type of religion among the cultivated and earnest youth of both sexes lacks moral nerve in lacking a due sense of that which (if I may say it) grew upon Christ as He drew to His crisis—the awfulness, the devilry, the inveteracy of evil. The great rally of the youth of this country to the war showed that they were better than much of their religion. There was a glorious atavism. The lack in the type of religion which is apt to prevail among clean and cultivated youth is due partly to some absence of human nature, some poverty of blood, and partly to defective insight into the final nature and victory of the Cross over the diabolism and perdition in the world. It reflects a certain moral amateurism due to the abeyance of a theology of the Cross. Such religion, certainly, loves the person of Christ. It is in love with His love, and with His Cross as the summit of that love in self-sacrifice. But it has no room nor need for judgment there. It does not feel there God's judgment on sin, and the crisis of the moral world and of a holy eternity. It needs moralising from a deeper experience of life—an experience older, more secular, more tragic. For want of a theology of conscience such souls do not know the world nor gauge its redemption. Their belief in Christ is impaired for want of a belief in the Satan that Christ felt it His supreme conflict to counterwork and destroy. This defect in the finer religion is likely to be repaired, and faith deepened and moralised by the rude shock given by the present war to a belief in human nature, and in a Christ that only appeals to human nature without judging it, a Christ that spiritualises rather than regenerates it, because He made more sacrifice for it than to God, and bore its load more than His judgment.

Many who think and speak much of the kingdom of God are yet averse to the idea of judgment in any sense as positive and distinctive as they find the social kingdom to be. They fasten on the kingdom as the message and task of Jesus, and they tend to deprecate the place once given to the Cross—as if Christ only died nobly, and did not die as King and justiciary of love's world. Yet at other seasons they speak as if they had everything in the Fatherhood of God. They do not observe that we cannot get the idea of a kingdom out of mere Fatherhood, but only the idea of a family; which, even when associated with the democratic idea (as in America), is quite inadequate to the dimensions and the destinies either of historic revelation or of historic humanity; and it may often in practice enfeeble religion for public effect. The sacred home and the sovereign people do not, even together, give us the social idea of Christianity, or they give one which does not rise above sociality, sunny piety, and delightful friendliness. It has not the altar at the centre of its worship. And at no great cost has it obtained its freedom. But the religion of the Mass will in the end be too much for this piety of the shining face if we have no more to go upon. The Father of Jesus was the Father in Heaven, the Father from above us all, the royal, the holy, the absolute Father, of an infinite majesty. And Christ went to His death in His function as King, not to become King. One of the compensatory boons of the present calamity of war may be to raise the whole moral pitch of religion out of the morass of sentimentalism, brisk or dreamy. And, among other things, it may reclaim for the absolute sovereignty of God, and the freedom of His grace, a place from which they have been ousted by a too individual, or domestic, or democratic, or egoist idea of Fatherhood. I say egoist, because there is a form of Christianity which makes everything (God included) minister to the worth of man, and renders nothing to the righteousness of God. It is humanist egoism. It is anthropocentric. And Christ was theocentric. Those to whom I have been alluding fail to see, first, that their fatherhood will not give the kingdom, and, second, that the kingdom carried with it the idea of judgment, and not sacrifice merely. Christ bore the love of God to men, but not without its element of wrath—the saving wrath of the Lamb. For that kingdom which was Christ's burthen the element of judgment is indispensable, since it was a holy kingdom. It is the function of a King reigning in eternal righteousness as it is not of a Father. It was certainly a supreme function of the kind of king which was present to an Oriental in Christ's day, and which He used much more than altered. For the God and Father of Jesus Christ was no more a president than a paterfamilias. The idea is not domestic but public. Even in the New Testament the idea of judgment precedes the establishment of the kingdom, is its negative coming, the left foot, as it were, in its march. Such, I say, was the current idea; and it was adopted by Christ for the soul, and carried through with a thoroughness that bewildered His disciples, even to betrayal and desertion. He carried it to the bitter end of the Cross and of the judgment both borne and exercised there. If we see the establishment of the kingdom in the Cross (and where else did Christ profess to set it up?), if Christ was there its true creative King and not its mere prophet, then in the Cross must lie also that element and principle of judgment. It is an element vital to Kingship and yet alien to many in whose Christianity the kingdom is more in evidence than in action, having never been worked in. That judgment—that, and not penalty—is the root of the whole doctrine of atonement—so unmistakably apostolic, however we may feel called to criticise it, or be tempted to hold it outgrown. It is the Self-justification of God in such a world as this.

In the Old Testament this Kingship certainly implied judgment in the interest of Israel as God's realm. And this again involved two things, one negative and one positive. It involved, first, the judgment of Israel's foes, and, second, Israel's justification, *i.e.* the public establishment of that righteousness for which Israel was to stand and suffer. Nay, further, there was involved a third thing—the judgment of Israel itself in the interest of that same righteousness. And this carried with it both the threshing out of a small remnant of the nation, and the use of the heathen as the divine flail.

We touch here a Scriptural note which to later days is somewhat strange. It is the note of a joy in judgment like the joy of harvest—the note so violently struck in Wordsworth's 'Carnage is God's Daughter.' The first idea of such judgment is associated with salvation, righteousness, and hope. God's peace is an end, not a beginning. The message is not peace and good-will among men; it is peace only for men disciplined into God's will, for men of such good-will. So the judgment which should do that was no mere day of wrath, no reign of terror, no storm of retribution, no taking of vengeance. It was a great hope. It was looked forward to and prayed for; it was promise more than doom. So much so, indeed, as to be in danger, in very popular hands, of becoming a matter of levity, with the day of the Lord no more than a Latin

Sunday, or *der Tag* of militarist savagery. That was one reason why the Prophets had to urge that it would sift even Israel. And this sifting was the beginning of that breach in the unity of the nation, and that crumbling of its solidary destiny, which issued in the individualism of its later days.

May I quote from myself? 'For the Bible as a whole, whether rising to the Cross or spreading from it, history is viewed under the category of judgment (though saving judgment) and not under that of progress. Eschatology goes much deeper than evolution. Only think of its moral nature rather than its sectorial form. The eschatologies are here in the true style of the Hebrew teleology of history. Its atmosphere was that of catastrophe and crisis rather than development. It thought of conversion, or regeneration, or restitution rather than of growth. The course of historic events is that of a series of judgments, each like an automatic release when the cup of iniquity was filled. But still it was an ascending series, rising from purification to redemption, through good men to prophets and through prophets to God's Son (Matt. xxi. 37). It was a long crescendo of judgment, ending in a crisis of all the crises, a harvest of all the harvests which had closed one age and begun a new, a grand climacteric of judgment, a last judgment, which dissipates for ever in a storm the silting up of all previous judgments, because ending a temporal world and opening an eternal. This was a time of terror, indeed, but far more a time of glory, since it meant the dawn of the kingdom more even than the doom of the world. As thought in the subject grew more individualist, it travelled beyond the plane even of history, and it drew the dead from Sheol in resurrection, to have justice done them, and to see the great justice done. So God fulfils and justifies Himself. The judgments of history, so far from calling for a theodicy, are parts of God's historic and practical theodicy. And they are so far from needing an apologia that, with such a world, the difficulty would be to defend God if they were not there.'

This idea of judgment was very current when Christ came ; and it coloured much of the first Christian preaching, through the turn it took from the expectation of Christ's speedy return, and through the way in which Apocalyptism took the lead of the old Prophetism. The new feature in Christianity was this—that the final judgment (whether as a historic, even cosmic, catastrophe, or as the close of each individual life) was effected in Jesus Christ, and consummated by Him (John v. 22). So much so that a great deal of Christian thought was given to the question how a future judgment of believers could comport with the facts of the Christian salvation, final and secure. The ideas of responsibility and retribution must be adjusted to the assurance of justification. The election of Israel and its pardon did not give it immunity from judgment. The end of the law in Christ did not destroy the final judgment, but it provided the final standard. The idea of a judgment is bound up with a moral order of a very real, immanent, and urgent, not to say eternal, kind. Yet how does it comport with grace ? Is the gracious God judge at all in His grace ? How can Christ be at once the living embodiment of the moral law (and so both standard and judge) and also the living grace of God and the agent of reconcilement ? This is the issue in the Cross, and for many it has been its offence. And the line of answer is that the grace is the judgment ; that grace, acting by way of atonement, has in its very nature a moral element, which does not leave the indifferent immune, but becomes their judgments. Judgment is the negative side of love's positive righteousness.

In the great and final inquest the judge is Christ the justifier. And the judgment falls on the Church and its faith, rather than on the world and its no faith. But it falls on the Church largely in respect of that which brings it into living and loving contact with the elemental human need (Matthew xxv. 31).[1] The same judgment is at once universal and individual. And for the individual there is no sound certainty of salvation, none beyond the risk of illusion, but that which will bear the test of a final judgment of moral finality (Matthew vii. 21). So 1 Cor. iv. 4. We may be judged at last (though not justified) by what may be below our own conscious motive. 'When saw we Thee an hungered?' We are to God more than we know. It is certainly not by atomic acts we are judged, nor by their balance tested by a mere law (1 Cor. iii. 15). The ultimate, the fundamental, judgment is an adjustment between persons—God's and man's. It is not between a soul and a law. It is a judgment of our faith and its personal relation to the true Christian, rather than of our works, which are the fruit of the relation. Lip confession of Christ is nothing; but soul confession, life confession, there must be. The great judgment is not upon works, but upon the standing life-act which

[1] With reference to Matthew xxv., it may be observed (though not without hesitation):

1. It concerns, perhaps, works of love to poor and afflicted Christians rather than to the poor of Humanity. The dividing line goes through the Church. Cf. Matthew vii. 21, 'Lord, Lord.' The heathen make but a background of spectators.

2. The ultimate value of the service is not its Humanitarianism, but its Christianity, its being done to Christ—done not out of humane pity but out of Christian faith, however indirectly—done not to men but to Christians, because Christians are the people in Christ's presence. The real final saving thing is the doer's relation to Christ. Inhumanity is not surprising in the natural man, but in a Christian man or people it is damnable.

3. This is not the sole thing which determines judgment. For Christ praises other qualities and virtues—as in the Beatitudes—and promises them blessedness. Hence this must have been 'occasional,' and must refer to a situation which demanded prominence for these philanthropies. Christians were not such because of this, but this is what showed if their faith was the true righteousness, the true relation to Christ.

practically and eternally disposes of the person. It is Rome's error to say that justification is by law, and that grace is merely to supply us with the power to keep the law after a free pardon of original sin in baptism. Obedience to Christ is the product of love and personal relation to Him (John xiv. 15 ; 1 John iv. 17, v. 3).

There is then a goal of history and a theodicy in the grand style ; and it is a last judgment (whatever form it take) according to God's grace. God vindicates Himself by a righteous grace. His answer to human sin was—Christ as crucified. The grace of God is the greatest judgment ever passed on the world. That is the nature of the Cross—God's grace (and not God's law), in moral, saving judgment on man. When we have entered the kingdom through the great judgment in the Cross, we do not escape all judgment ; we escape into a new kind of judgment, from that of law to that of grace. We escape condemnation, for we are new creatures, but chastisement we do not escape. Our work may be burned, to our grief, that we may be saved (1 Cor. xi. 32). We are judged or chastened with the Church to escape condemnation with the world. And at the last must there not be some great crisis of self-judgment, when we all see Him as He is, and see ourselves as His grace sees us ?

The modern interest in judgment is not in a last judgment that ends history. That may be too far off to be effective, and the damages too remote. But we are concerned about the action of the judgment principle in history and the soul. We are concerned in an inmost and ineluctable judgment active in experience ; in an ultimate and absolute judgment which, rising from the last centre to the surface, slowly and subtly pervades and controls it; a moral purpose taking historic effect in affairs in its unhurried but inevitable way. This is what might be called the intra-worldly action of Christ's Cross, and it is one which the Church has too much neglected. It is to many an incredible, and even unintelligible, thing to say that the last judgment took place in principle in that Cross as God's last word and Self-vindication to the world, that we are living in the midst of it, and that all history is working it into detail, whether by way of order or of convulsion. Nor are they less bewildered when they are told that the thing which took place on that Cross was a tragedy and a crisis infinitely greater than if Germany plunged every State into war, if America were submerged in the ocean, or Britain cast into the depths of the sea; that it was a tragedy in which the holy heart of the loving God was more concerned than in the collapse of a whole civilisation. The Cross was a more momentous thing for God and history than the debacle of the Hittite, Babylonian, or Roman Empire. For He has seen them rise and set, but still the Cross leads His kingdom on. That Cross is not only very real but fontal, creative and final for the Kingdom of God to which all history moves. The act of saving judgment there, in the Cross, is not simply the historic summit of the moral order but the constant spiritual source of it. The Cross enacts on an eternal scale the moral principle which is subduing all history at last to itself and its holy love. The judgment *process* in history only unfolds the finality of the eternal judgment *act* which is in the Cross, to recondense it in the final settlement of all things. The kingdom of the world and the adventures of men are all under law to this Christ crucified and risen. Not one of them escapes from His leash, however long it may seem. That is the New Testament faith. And so long as Christianity remains our creed, so long will the Biblical idea remain which treats history as the prize of the Cross, the field of its ethic, the area of God's judgments, the constant upcasting to the top of the last judgment at the core; or, reversing this image, the penetration and settlement of His kingdom into the heart of affairs. For the Cross of Christ is not only set up in history, it takes root in it. Its very radicles split the rocks of time, so that they crumble into soil which feeds it. It is integrated into history, and weaves all historic vicissitudes into the judgment unto salvation. We are doomed to the greatness of Christ, and not merely wooed. The central interest of the world is its moral crisis. It is the crisis of its sin. And that is the eternal crisis of the Cross, the acme of the war in heaven. The Cross of Christ is God's last judgment on all sin, for its destruction by a realm of infinite grace and love. It is the last resource of the Almighty Holiness; and *His* last resource is the end of all things—which is now always at hand in a kingdom both coming and come. Only if God's saving love fail the world can judgment fail from the earth, only if He abandon it with His personal presence, and if His Self-revelation cease to be His historic Self-donation and Self-justification to the world. For God is not the Custodian of a moral order independent of Him, whose establishment is His mission in life. But He is His own kingdom, if we may put it so. And in His holiness we live, and move, and have our moral being at our last and best.

Hence the judgment on mankind is not so much a matter of ripening stages of moral progress (though these have their place), but it is rather the standing dilemma of the soul, single or social, its constant 'either—or,' for a holy God or no God in affairs, for God or for His enemies. Actually the line is not sharp, but really it is. Morally it is not, religiously it is. It is like the equator. We cannot trace it on the earth, but we cannot work without it. In the last resort judgment is not the realisation by stages of an idea, but a relation, an action, and a business between person and person, for or against. It is a matter of holy love, the gracious love of the Cross, taken as the constitutive principle of the world and the subduing, shaping principle of its history.

Yet, though it is not wholly untrue to say that *die Weltgeschichte ist das Weltgericht* it is not wholly true. It certainly needs to be supplemented. I hope to do this in my next chapter, but I will touch it now.

It is not the course, nor even the progress, of the world that is its judgment, but its invasion by Eternity, which, as holy, has in a Person the standard and the power of eternal moral value. The world's judgment is at a vital point and crisis of history, where God comes to stay and to work onward, where the eternal standard is set up for ever in the only form appropriate to the holy—in a living, loving, holy person in power. It is in Christ; and it is in that in Christ for which He was most concerned—the moral crisis, the holy judgment, and gracious salvation of all history by His Cross. All in Him gathered to the Passion; and in the Passion all gathered there, in judgment unto salvation. The key is not in process, and not in ideals, nor in their evolution, but in crisis, in an intervention, an invasion, a miracle of fundamental and final and holy grace, which from the first underlay all, but had to break through all. The reconciliation of the world with God, the judgment of its conscience (which is its painful adjustment) by His holy love, is effected in the central act of the Cross; the act of a judgment which meant not only effect given to God's holy love, but also separation made between those who chose it and those who did not. And of this real, ultimate, moral judgment, the holy God's last word in the way of His estimate and treatment of the world, the last judgment so called, is but the consummation in actual detail. It sets forth a judgment already in principle effected and put in conquering action among the forces of history by the ever-sifting Gospel and the touchstone of grace. What is judgment but the setting out in true and full light (*i.e.* in just relation to the whole) of the actual state of things between the soul's case and the ruling power of the world ? Unless Christ be a dream or a dreamer, that power is God's grace. That is our final judge. To it we stand or fall. The gospel of grace, in the Cross and its preaching, is the real ultimate judgment of the world, the real and final power at work *now*. When the world is brought to book, the book is neither a celestial code nor a log kept by recording angels. It is the Bible as the shrine of the Gospel. Its Cross is the historic bench, as it were, on which Christ sits as Judge and Saviour. There is no appeal from that Court and that verdict. We must all stand (and all means at last) before the judgment-seat of Christ crucified. The one moral crisis of the world is there—unless we strip from the Cross the notion of either world judgment or atonement, and make it but a piece of æsthetic sacrifice, or moving appeal, or ingenious retrieval in a backwater of history. The curse of orthodoxy, and of the current religion it has coloured, has been to sever the Cross from the whole moral fabric and movement of the universe and make it a theologian's affair. To the Cross conscience stands or falls to the Cross as the moral crisis of souls, of nations, of the universe, and of Eternity. The belief in a last judgment is much more than good for the soul ; a last, a fundamental, judgment is the very genius both of God's dominion and of the salvation in love of all souls. A final judgment on the soul is one also on the world. Death only removes us from earthly conditions, not from this Christ—rather from the distance between us and Him ; and it is only when all the world stands before Christ, only as we have such a Christ as draws the world by its conscience to His bar, that each man is finally judged to his saved place.

Without the judgment and destiny effected in the Cross of Christ we can have no teleology of history. This is a thing that a philosophy of history cannot give. It cannot deal with the evil that is in the world. It cannot assure us that the holy will win the day at last. We do not receive the end in advance, as Christian faith does. We may be more or less able to cherish a general optimism, but we do not really discover a moral teleology in things, because we do not discover the telos, sure, subtle, ubiquitous, and almighty. We do not have a Christ who is the end in the beginning. We are not presented with a starting point for our faith, with God's own principle of a final judgment. We search the heavens of the past without a pole or a sun, and we see but fanciful constellations of history instead of divine orbits and systems. The very last judgment on things, we think, is yet to come, it is not come already. And we are not yet told its principle. God has not said His last word with the world. We can never be sure, for instance, that in a great war the issue will go to the side that has most justice, or that most makes for the kingdom of God. It might go to military efficiency, to the side that has the best machine and the least scruple. And, failing such assurance, we have no point of revelation which gives us in one act the ground of to-day and the goal of to-morrow, which presents us in advance with the purpose and destiny of the world, and which enables us, by a holy spirit breaking free from the coteries, to divine the object of all history working up through it. We are afraid that if we find that moral ground and destiny of the world in the historic Christ and His Cross, and if we say 'we see not yet all things put under righteousness, but we see Jesus,' and rest, we shall be called Biblicists instead of historians, more theological than ethical. Well, we must take the risk. The judgment of the world accordingly is not the history of the world, but its Saviour. There is judgment in history, but the verdict of history is not the whole of judgment. At any stage it is but partial, and success is not settlement. It all runs out and runs up into a last judgment, and the reconstitution of all things. God judges the world as He brings all men to their last stand and hope—before Christ the first and the last. He judges the world as He comes in Christ to all men. The judgment of the world has therefore much to do, and closely, with missions to the world. Christian universalism turns on a belief, not in the unity of Humanity (which we cannot be sure of), but in the one final Goal and Judge and Saviour and King of all men. It is by the conscience that mankind is one by its witness of the one power over it; and Christ gathers up the conscience of the race, and, in His own Soul, sets it in the active light of the conscience of God. To a holy God the salvation of the world's evil soul is a matter of conscience.

We are all standing before the judgment-seat of Christ. And one day we shall know it. We end where we began —in Him. All things are set at last in that light. His love—our great boon or else our great doom—is the deep and cryptic formula of the movement of Time. Time is great with that Eternity. But its process is no mere metamorphosis of Humanity by the progress of humane civilisation, philanthropy, and social reform—inevitable as it makes such things to be. Love is not simply the great propelling and enriching principle; it is the great discriminating, consuming, selective, reconstitutive principle. Its holiness is the principle of sifting, and creative and redemptive judgment. The consummation does not arrive with the gradual leavening and organisation of Humanity by the law of sympathetic love. It is more creative than that, and more of a gift from above, more of a holy justification. It goes back at every point for its source and power to the decisive, finished, ultimate, and eternal act of the God of holy love in His Cross. It comes as this ceaseless Act works up through all things in a creative evolution to their control, taking effect, taking selective, rejecting, condemning, saving effect in history, and guiding or forcing every soul upon its moral relation to the redemption of Eternity far more than to the ameliorations of Time. The Christian word of the Cross is not that God is love, but that God's love as holy is the omnipotence of the world with the final reversion of all things.

So the justification of God is not given us by Christ; it *is* Christ; who under the judgment from man took His native place as the judge of all the earth, justifying the God of holy love in His justification of all the world.

CHAPTER XI

HISTORY AND JUDGMENT

I

Scriptural

It has always been the bane of theology when it has been isolated from the course of public affairs, and left neutral to the issues of history—when it has been other-worldly. This brought Lutheranism to the sterile orthodoxy of the seventeenth century, and has now reduced it to a living death in its Byzantinism in the twentieth ; while the opposite course, a practical and inner-worldly interest in the kingdom of God, has made Calvinism the religious creator of the free and humane West. The severance has also affected American religion, to say nothing of British. Doctrine and politics are far from neutral, when our scale of survey is duly wide.

But there are junctures in history which much affect the perspective of belief, and draw into light certain doctrines rather than others. In the days of rampant individualism it was necessary to emphasise the *love* of God to supply the sympathetic and binding note. But now, when the unit is taken in hand by such a machinery of social organisation and efficiency as the world has never seen, and when the love of God has fallen to mean but natural affection magnified, the faith of a spiritual and holy power is carried home by *judgment*. Such efficiency, being on a scale no larger than national egoism, has issued in militarism and war—cynic, ethic, and ruthless war; and so God takes His own text, and preaches, to those that have ears to hear, judgment. His great sermons on crucial occasions are long, and deeply theological. Perhaps now we may grow in the mood to listen, and the skill to read His signs in the times. What is the Christian theology of public judgment? It is not great nations only, but modern civilisation that is at the bar. Does it stand before the judgment-seat of Christ?

In the Bible, in Christianity, the idea of judgment is not that of a remote and unearthly *dies iræ*—a notion which has become a demoralising dream, withdrawing religion from the midst of life. Judgment is the visitation of a Saviour. It comes into affairs. It means less destruction than reconstitution. It has a note of joy in it, the joy of harvest. (Cp. Psalm xcvi.) It is associated with salvation, public righteousness, and endless hope. A salvation without judgment is not thought of, nor a judgment without salvation. It is a function of the Great King, and the obverse of the Great Kingdom.

For the Bible as a whole, history, rising to the Cross and spreading from it, is viewed under this category of saving judgment, and not that of civilised progress. The atmosphere is one of dilemma, choice, and crisis rather than development. The thought is that of a destiny reached by conversion, regeneration, or restitution, rather than growth. Evil comes to a head, sin is precipitated into transgression (Rom. vii.), that it may be dealt with centrally, and with more or less finality. But yet this scriptural idea of judgment and crisis is not quite incompatible with more modern views of history. As room has been found for both creation and development in Bergson's *Creative Evolution*, so we may adjust the old truth and the new in respect of judgment. We recognise an evolution of crises. The last judgment is the last of a long train, and the series is an ascending series (Matt. xxi. 37). It is a crescendo of judgment, ending in a crisis of all the crises, a harvest of all the harvests which had gathered up one age and begun a new, a grand climacteric of judgment, closing one world, opening another, and dissipating for ever in a storm the silting up of all previous junctures. But it always means the dawn of the kingdom more than the doom of the world. And as thought grew more individualist it travelled outside visible history, and drew the dead from Sheol in resurrection, to have justice done them and to see justice done.

This notion of judgment was very current when Christ came; and it coloured much Christian preaching through the expectation of Christ's speedy return. The new feature in Christianity was this—that the final judgment was closely associated, and even identified, with the work of the historic Christ. It was in principle effected in Jesus Christ, and consummated by Him. He died as King. His work of the Cross was the world's judgment unto its salvation. It was God's final treatment of the world. We shall face it at the end; but only because now we face it at bottom. The 'last judgment' is but a time expression of this ultimate judgment, now inherent, perpetual, and fundamental. Ever since, human history has been living in this final judgment, and living it out. Nothing in history or the soul comes to its true end without finding its judgment in Christ. 'To live is Christ.' And the great judgment is His grace.

II

Evangelical

It is the mark of the Dark Ages and the Church's millennial slumber that theology departed from its historic base and lost the sense of history in the wilds of speculation. This base and this sense we are only now recovering for faith. The first Christian principle was right, whatever we think of its first form. High history is not possible without the teleology which a final judgment supplies for all other crises. And Christianity alone, by this article of faith, makes a history of the world possible. It restores theology to history, and history to theology. But it must be a much more deep, realist, and urgent theology than has been current in the popular religion, now so rudely shattered.

The principle of a final judgment means an incessant and fundamental judgment, and not merely a terminal; it is immanent and not remote. It is a finality working in history, not after it. And the course of history is such, especially present history, that without a revelation of the kind it would be impossible to believe in a moral control of the large career of events. Such a revelation gives us the divine movement, measure, and destiny of the world; and it declares this moral *nisus* (whose climacteric is the Cross) to be working, dominant however latent, in all things that are done. Christ died as King of the world. He is the perpetual chief of the Great Powers, whose true balance is His control. This view fertilises all our recent progress in anthropology and history, because it gives such things their true reference to Eternity, and their organic continuity with it at every point, however deeply the connecting lines are laid out of sight. But it implies a Christ whose royal action, and especially whose reconciliation, was, above all things moral, moral more than affectional,[1] moral with the mystic ethic of Eternity. This moral action, re-creating the race in the heart of its affairs, has its focal point in the holy Cross, *i.e.* in a Cross ruled by the eternal, ethical conditions of holy love, and of salvation by its judgment. If Time is related at every point to a holy Eternity, to the kingdom of a holy God

[1] 'Be ye *reconciled*—for He hath made Him to be *sin* for us who knew no sin that we might be made the *righteousness* of God in Him.'

and not a mere national Deity, it must be related in a way of final judgment, of moral crisis and settlement, and not of endless evolution or transfiguration. For holiness is action, and not mere process. Such was the Cross of Christ. The judgment principle, searching, sifting, parting to right and left, to life and death, settling all things, slowly setting up an eternal kingdom, and not merely moving onwards like a civilisation, was within all that Christ was, and at last did.[1] The mode of salvation was judgment, since it was atonement. We still find that an indifference as to any final judgment is common where the Cross is softened to exclude the idea of atoning judgment. And the apathy works out into a disbelief of judgment radical and ubiquitous, into a light sense of spiritual wickedness in high places, and into the moral cynicism and cruelty of the natural man as statesman or man of the world. That indifference is the symptom of a state of things in which the Cross loses its searching and universal, its ethical and public quality, and comes to be admired as heroic sacrifice, or sweetened to the taste of the piety of religious groups.

There is no side of theology (we have seen) on which the age is so exercised and so bewildered as in the matter of a theodicy—a vindication of the ways of God among men, especially on a large and public scale. That need was perhaps never felt as it is in this dreadful day. But (we have also seen) without the revelation of a final judgment, a judgment final both in future time and present principle, no theodicy is possible. Where shall we find that revelation? It cannot be traced in affairs but only trusted in Christ. We cannot discover a God of holy love in the career of history so far as gone, nor in the principles of a rational idealism; we can but meet Him at the point where it pleased Him to appear as Saviour, and greet Him at the historic spot He chose, to

[1] Every Beatitude was balanced by a Woe, as in Luke's version.

set for ever His name and nature there. Our belief in God, historic as it is, is a belief in spite of history. Those who draw their belief from God's treatment of them or their time must collapse in the black hour. It is not wonderful if, in the present awful juncture, a belief which grew up but in fine weather should go to pieces on moral grounds. It is the Cross amid history that saves us from history—by enacting God's last judgment in history, and providing the moral key to its otherwise impenetrable cipher. The practical abeyance, for the age's religion, of faith in a final judgment (whether fundamental or terminal) concurs with the loss of a ruling faith in God's judging action in the long orbits of public affairs. Along with a faith in the Great Inquest, the faith in the reign of righteousness subsides, sinking to patriotism as religion, and to the belief in world-mastery by brute force in scientific hands. With the faith in a moral consummation at last, effected by a holy God rather than developed by man's conscience, there sinks the faith in a moral order immanent now, with any native right, intrinsic promise, or eternal value; and we become the victims of a moral relativism with no absolute principle, with no rock of ages, but only a spirit of the age.

It is a common but vain inquiry whether the balance in the world at any given time is for good or evil, whether the amount of actual good in any age or stage exceeds the amount of evil in it. We cannot tell—the quantitative scale being here out of place—nor would it profit much to know. What we must know is, which is destined to conquer, which is on its way to conquer, however unmarked, which has the reversion of the world, and has it on the guarantee of the Ruler of a world overcome already. Does the mastery by civilisation of the sensible world (which we *can* trace) connote and ensure also our mastery of the moral? Is efficiency the warrant of salvation? The most favourable answers of the best thinkers on such questions do not go beyond probabilities—which events like those now round us reduce for some minds to vanishing point. So that pessimism, with final debacle, is erected into a creed, upon the debris of the creeds of hope. So ends a religion of probabilities. For faith we must have facts, and facts eternal and sure. We must have a fact which ensures all the future because it contains it, creates it, and gives us the final settlement of the moral soul in advance. For Christian faith (be it right or wrong) that fact is Christ's Cross, as a greater fact than all history, for which now all history moves. He is the last judgment, yesterday, to-day, and for ever, the goal and justification of all the devious, dreadful ways of earth. The deepest thing, whether in progress or catastrophe, is its contribution to His denouement. Christ in His Cross is the theodicy of history, its crisis, its essential, and final, and glorious justice. Things are so profoundly out of joint that only something deeper than the wrecked world can mend them, only a God of love and power infinite, making his sovereignty good once for all, though mountains are cast into the sea. The only theodicy is not a system, but a salvation; it is God's own saving Act and final judgment, incarnate historically and personally. The Cross of Christ, eternal and universal, immutable and invincible, is the moral goal and principle of nations and affairs. If it seem ridiculous to say that a riot and devilry of wickedness like the present war is still not out of the providence of Christ's holy love, it is because we are victims of a prior unfaith. It is because we have come to think it a theological absurdity to say that the Cross of Christ outweighs for God in awful tragedy, historic moment, and eternal effect a whole world ranged in inhuman arms. We do not really believe that it is Christ, 'crucified to the end of the world' (as Pascal says), that pays the last cost for all parties of this war. That God spared not His own Son is a greater shock to the natural conscience than the collapse of civilisation in blood would be. For civilisation may deserve to collapse, if only because it crucified the Son of God, and crucifies Him afresh. But if God spared not His own Son, He will spare no historic convulsion needful for His kingdom. And if the unspared Son neither complained nor challenged, but praised and hallowed the Father's name, we may worship and bow the head.

III

Philosophical

The Church, with a last judgment remote, and an individualist salvation by private bargain at hand, has much failed in relating the Cross to history. And in so far it has been untrue to its Bible.

Apocalyptic, which started in prophecy, regains the ethical note in the apostles. It has been abundantly shown by scholars that even in the New Testament itself the process of thought had begun in which the eschatological is converted into the ethical, and the real action of judgment withdrawn from a future convulsion to be pressed into the moral present. But this moralising of history was soon lost, and lost long. And one of the services of the Illumination was to recover it in a measure. This recuperative tendency has grown; and during the last century it went so far that the balance has been lost in the other direction, and belief in a great final judgment, or of a second coming of Christ, to wind up history, has been relegated to certain obscurantist sections of the Church which still cherish chiliastic dreams. Christ, it is said, is returning here and now, in the fruitions or nemeses of history. This is a valuable creed; but as it is preached it is part of a general tendency to substitute historic process for divine purpose and action. And the result has been in many cases to destroy the idea of judgment altogether, here or hereafter—as has happened through the practical loss of the idea of an endless hell, or indeed of any. Or, at best, the result has been to substitute for God's judgment the self-assertion of a mere moral order, and that chiefly in the more negative and retributory way.

But the chief lack is not the absence of that positive and constructive element in judgment which makes it the growing pains of the kingdom as it comes; it is the absence, not so much of the idea of present judgment, but of its finality in a kingdom come. By which I mean this.

No doubt it is much gained to be clear that judgment is not deferred to a time so distant that its practical influence cannot cross the intervening gulf. It is well that the idea should be destroyed which makes damages so remote that the vigorous and scientific sinner can go on to sin with defiant impunity and confidence. It is well that we should know that, as men or nations, we are daily registering our own judgment in the character our conduct is laying down, that we are creating our own Kharma, that we are writing two copies of our life at once—one of them, through the black carbon of time and death, in the eternal. And it elevates the whole conception of history to view it as at bottom the action, almost automatic, and therefore certain, of the divine judgment—so long as we can rise to think it is moral *action* with an end, and not merely incessant moral *process*. All that is to the good. But the tendency is to lose, in the moral automatism, the sense of judgment as more than sure nemesis, as the work of a living and saving God who has already said His last and endless word in this kind. We tend to miss in judgment the incessant reaction of His personal and absolute holiness as the last creative power in all being, and the organising principle of its slow evolution through time. We are led to think more of the judgment than of the Judge. It then becomes hard, very often, to believe in judgment, or trace the justice at work at all. And we come out of the welter, perhaps, with little more at best than a general faith that there is a distinction between right and wrong, possibly even a fundamental one, but with no assurance which will win at last, whether the far end of it all will be a kingdom of God or a kingdom of Satan.

But surely it is clear that if history is to be read teleologically at all, the telos cannot be reached by an induction from small areas of the past, far less from our individual experience. Nor, indeed, can it be won from the whole past, which may be but a small area of the whole of time. Besides, we need a principle of selection among the multitude and variety of past facts to begin with. Nor can we have that telos in a mere intuition of the present, a mere power of piercing the chaos of the newspapers, and reaching the idea by the just insight of genius. For this, like all the intuitions and mysticisms, however fine, is but aristocratic and for the few. And though genius can do much in that penetrating way, it has not yet given us the principle of the final judgment on things, Heaven's last relation to Earth. That lies deeper than genius can go. Genius proceeds from us rather than descends on us. The insight of genius does not rise to revelation of the Eternal. It realises man rather than reveals God. It is a part of nature rather than of God—nature returning on itself to interpret itself, rather than God giving Himself in revelation once for all. Nature, even in genius, cannot explain itself either in its origin or destiny. It gives us certainty neither about infinite God nor finite man. The last principle of things lies with religion, and with the creative revelation of grace at the root of it. Universality and finality go together in Christ, in whose 'finished work' we are presented with all the future in advance. A real revelation like His gives us the end in the beginning.

Grace is the last word of omnipotence, as the collect greatly says. The principle of immanent and ultimate and saving judgment, and of reconciliation by judgment, is, therefore, the principle of the Cross of Christ as *the* moral crisis of God and man, *i.e.* of the universe. This is the principle both of the closing judgment in time and of the fundamental judgment going on timelessly within history and character. All moves to the holy (*i.e.* the mystically moral) reconciliation in Christ, as the final settlement of all things and all souls. That is what is being distilled for eternity out of the long process of time.

It is quite true that neither revelation nor book is there to give us a panorama of the past or a programme of the future. It is in no such sense that judgment is revealed. The Bible is not a sketch-book of past things nor a picture-book of the last things. It has been especially discredited by treating its imaginative symbols of the future as if they were specifications or working plans attached to God's new covenant and contract with man. That is the bane of a direct and popular Biblicism. But, for all that, Christianity can never give up faith in the gift to us in advance of an immanent teleology of history, whose principle was secured (and not illustrated) in the Cross, and to whose consummation history moves as the kingdom of God set up there. Christianity does believe in a solution already real, however unseen. We now live amid the evolution of the final crisis and last judgment of the sempiternal Cross. All the moral judgment moving to effect in the career of souls, societies, and nations is the action of the Cross as the final, crucial, eternal Act of the moral power of the universe.

The bane of popular Christianity is that it has severed the Cross from the moral principle for which the world is built, from the creative leaven in active things, and has made it a second best, a supplementary device for the rescue of a section of mankind who occupy to it a certain relation of greater or less piety. Salvation, the Church, the kingdom become but the proceeds from a good sale of the wreck of creation. Our theories of regeneration, baptismal and other, rob the new creation of its commanding relation to the first. For, if we will be thorough, in the new birth creation itself is created anew, and not merely its wreck; and it is created more creatively, and not only as the last phase of the first. Regeneration is mightier creation. Yet the Cross has been made but a valuable religious expedient, instead of the universal and creative principle of the moral soul. From being the judgment focus of absolute righteousness in all things it has become but an oasis and a spring far to one side of the great journey of the race. We have come to regard it not as the moral power but as rescue from the moral power; because the idea of judgment has been either distorted in the historic Cross or dislodged from it. This severance of the Gospel from public history and social affairs, its monopoly by individualism, sectionalism, and pietism, has made Evangelicalism a byword of national impotence, by reducing the ardour of the kingdom for many to no more than a devout interest in propaganda, home or foreign, to its extensive rather than its intensive culture. To carry the Cross into the world has often meant no more than carrying it abroad; carrying it into life no more than personal piety in the shape of resignation or self-sacrifice—with the result that the one becomes negative and the other indiscriminate, for lack of a moral end identical with the object of faith. The Cross is not mere submission; and self-sacrifice has in itself no moral value, since all turns on the object and principle of its obedience. Obedience is better than sacrifice; and some who are voluble of sacrifice we might wish more prolific of duty. The Cross is not there to kindle a passion of altruism but to moralise self-sacrifice, and to save it from itself by its reference to the first principle of religion—the holy. Yet the Cross of Christ is not merely the holy summit of the moral order. *Sub specie æternitatis*, it is its creative source. And it is the active principle which slowly brings to book the devices of men, the enterprises of heroes, and the adventures of nations. It is a creative revolution, which inverts the values that fired their passion and converts to God's kingdom their egoist schemes. It is the judgment-bar of the mystic, eternal, and immutable morality.

IV

Critical

These observations may be illustrated by reference to the famous phrase of Schiller which, I will say at once, represents one of the most valuable gifts of last century to the conception of history—more valuable than Lessing's view of it as the education of the race. *Die Weltgeschichte ist das Weltgericht* ('History is the true criticism and last judgment of the world') is a great word. But it may hide in it also a great fallacy. It may easily come to mean what is so false in recent pragmatism—that efficiency is the test of right, that only clear fitness survives, that nothing is to be held true till you see it works, that the only success is success. It does not do justice to the Christian idea. At first, indeed, it seems to give the Bible principle an immense expansion; and it did, as the Bible was then understood. It was a very necessary protest, in the interest of moral realism, against the current other-worldliness of the judgment idea. It does much to make the historic process a moral one, to ethicise history, to carry the principle of judgment into the order of the day, and make it an inevitable, searching presence from which we cannot escape, because we cannot escape from ourselves, or discard our moral psychology. It seems to infuse righteousness into the soul's history and the course of affairs. So it seems. And in some ways so it does. It certainly recalls us from melodramatic pictures of a judgment far off, and therefore morally faint and negligible. But is it all gain to lock eternity up in the time process, to quash the appeal from time's crude justice to eternity, to lose from earth's judgment the idea of heaven's finality and the verve of the soul's eternal dilemma ? Does it not lose that reference to a present eternity which makes judgment a part of real religion ? And, granting that history is a moral process, are we left quite sure that it is goodness that is working up and working out to the final control ? Is the idea of a moral entail or nemesis the chief idea in judgment ? Is there nothing more creative ? Is man's pursuit by nemesis really an educative influence at the last ? Is not mere punishment morally stupefying ? And is it otherwise if only happiness ensue and prosperity ? Did not even Judaism outgrow that idea ? Is the idea of a moral filiation of events, an ethical causation without end—is that judgment ? Are we not left at the mercy of an endless relativism, where white is only the lightest shade of black ? What did they found on who believed before the results of faith came in and believed to such purpose in making them come in ? Are there not two great elements lacking here which are essential to the idea of judgment—the element of reconstitution, *i.e.* of redemption or reconciliation, as something greater than progress, and the element of finality, as the moral postulate of an absolute standard ? The ethical process in mere history has no real closes. The books are never made up. To what does it all move ? What is the goal whose creative emergence all along makes the career ? Can we say that Schiller's phrase implies the importation of divine righteousness into the career of things ? How do we know that the nexus or the bias of the moral causation in history is righteousness at bottom ? How do we know that it is more than eudemonist ? What is righteousness ? How can we be sure that the world process means righteousness, till we either reach the end, or receive a revelation which gives us the end in advance—in any case, without a luminous crisis decisive for the holy and for ever ? The phrase suggests that judgment consists in no more than an event entails inevitably, by moral causation, within the historic field, wide or narrow. But by the time this comes home both sinner and saint are beyond its reach, and it falls on an innocent posterity. Does the judgment for a wicked war fall but on those it damages, and miss its promoters ? History may have moral value, and not only scientific connections ; it may be a practical criticism of moral ideas ; but it is not a criterion of moral values. Nor is it the judge of moral souls, which contain more than they can ever put into external effect. The phrase, I say, does not supply the principle of an active teleology. The virtue which approves itself may not be sufficient to establish itself. It may wrap itself in its robe of stoic righteousness, but it does not cast its mantle over the world, and it seems to give away the infinite moral value of the individual soul ; which is an end in itself, which history cannot read, which was made to rest in an Oversoul, and which, for good or ill, is too great to find its full expression and effect, or to have justice done it, in history, however prolonged.

It is all part of the Hegelian tendency to find finality in the moving idea, and to set up a theodicy more reasonable than religious, because judgment is diffused in history as a rational process instead of being condensed in God's personal Act at a crucial, positive point, creating our act of faith in the face of history. It also destroys the conception of judgment as a personal relation and crisis, and it hands us over to the rule of abstract and will-less law in the moral world of wills. It corresponds in ethics to monism in the cosmos. Such a view really abolishes the idea of judgment as eternity subduing time, except in so far as the evolving idea may be viewed as eternity. It discards for serial process the personal and dramatic notion of crisis. It drops us to a moving series of integrations and eliminations, with no law but causation, no values but those that are relative, and no standard to measure whether movement is progress, or evolution is development to any end. We have none of that invasion and control of time by eternity which is so lacking in 'progress,' and yet is so necessary for the idea of real growth. It gives us no gift and no faith of a final goal of reconciliation, whose emergence makes all the process right and all worth while. It destroys, of course, the idea of a last judgment accessible in time and decisive in eternity; and it thus takes the momentous note of finality, standard, and repose out of the higher life. The more wide our knowledge the less is anything final, the more is everything relative; even evil is but good in the making. In seeming to ethicise history it turns its action into a procession of principles devouring persons; and so it really lowers the dramatic quality, the critical gravity, and the moral value both of history and life. It co-operates with the loss of faith in a real judgment by Christ's Cross to reduce the moral temperature even amidst ethical ardours, to quench moral insight in mere ethical interest, to starve the idea of holiness, and therefore blanch the idea of evil. It tends to make the real seriousness of salvation unintelligible, to produce disciples rather than converts, confessors, or apostles, and to lower the worth of Christ to a spiritual influence or ideal that would not essentially suffer if the Cross were lopped from His life. All that is implied in a phrase like 'the fullness of time,' vanishes in a process which seems infinitely expansive but is really levelling, with a horizon but no content nor crisis. It widens the area of the moral monotony in mere process by turning judgment from the vital act of a person to the quick march of ideas. To live may be growth, but it is not Christ. Life grows more complex but more discursive, more busy but more meaningless, more involved but involving less. It ramifies infinitely, and crystallises not at all. It has nothing to crystallise on. It is an elaborate tale signifying nothing final or eternal—endless differentiation, but what satisfaction? It becomes a thing of infinite *nuances*, grades, variations, discriminations of coarse and fine, more or less, and so forth, but not of good and evil, not their grand and eternal dilemma, which, after all, makes possible moral choice, moral dignity, and life's responsible value. Life becomes more æsthetic than ethical. God is superfluous, or at best the Trustee and Executor of a moral order which is easily thought of as detachable from Him; and we are then the victims of moral law, and not the objects of moral redemption. The moral law itself may then sink from something human to something which is but egoism, individual or national—as among the combatants in the war we hear loud appeals to a tutelary God, but entire silence about Christ, His judgment, or His kingdom. The nations, relapsing into Hebraism at best and Paganism at worst, lose the world-Christ in a tribal God.

V

Ironical

In many cases in life the important thing is not what is said but what is not said. That is what the experienced man is most concerned to interpret. That is what he comes either to distrust or to rely on most. When we have to reckon men up, or to revise our interviews with them, we may attach most weight not to the words we heard but to the one remark we expected but it did not come. It is so in nature. The stillness of the night often seems more full and more impressive than the bustle of the day. Its calm is a rebuke, or at least a monition, to the day's passion and the day's haste; the repose is full of subtle question. So as we rise in the scale and business of life the silence may be more eloquent and even active than the sound; and more is meant by reserve than by response. The criticism by silence can be as severe as any.

God's judgment on things and in things is not absent because it is still, and it is not out of action because it is not obvious nor obtrusive. The Gnostics found in the Silence the Fullness. There is a judgment which is not visitation but irony. Its tarrying works upon us more than its coming. It enlists our imagination as its ally. It broods evasive, provoking, potent. If God do not yet intervene on earth He sits in heaven—sits and laughs. And His smile is inscrutable, and elusive, only not cruel: the smile of endless power and patience, very still, and very secure, and deeply, dimly kind. The judgment of God can be as lofty and sleepless as the irony of heaven over earth, or the irony of history upon earth. 'Thou didst deceive me and I was deceived.' Heine spoke daringly of the Aristophanes of heaven. But that is not the smile that any Christian can see or credit over us. Yet it need not be either faithless or foolish to speak of the Socratic heavens. God seems so slow, so clouded, so fumbling in His ways; and His questions that do reach us seem so irrelevant, so naïve—but they are so dangerous. The powers that delay but do not forget are not simple, impotent, or confused as they tarry. If fire do not fall from the heavens they yet rain influence down. There is a world of meaning in their gaze upon men whom they do not yet smite. It is neither a stony nor a bovine stare. All the world is being summed up by that bland sky.

Its light is invisibly actinic on earth. What seems distance and irrelevance, weak and unweeting, may well put us on our guard. The heavens are not so simple as they seem, nor is God so mocked as He consents to appear, and to appear for long. He gives our desire, and it shrivels our soul. Of our pleasant vices He is making instruments to scourge us. The passions, ambitions, and adventures of men go on to achieve their end through a riot of worldliness, wickedness, defiance, and guilt; but they are after all the levers for a mightier purpose than theirs, which thrives on their collapse. The wrath of man works the righteousness of God. Satan's last chagrin is his contribution to God's kingdom. The great agents of the divine purpose have often no idea of it. 'Cyrus, my servant.' One thing they do with all their might, but God accomplishes by them quite another. Julius Cæsar never intended nor conceived the Roman Church; but it came by him, and he was murdered. His ambition was his death, but his great function was a thing vaster than the Roman Empire. There is a certain truth (if we will be very careful with it) in the early Christian fantasy that Satan was befooled by the patient naïveté of Christ. This is the irony of history—when the very success of an idea creates the conditions that belie it, smother it, and replace it. Catholicism becomes the Papacy. The care for truth turns to the Inquisition. The religious orders, vowed to poverty, die and rot of wealth. A revival movement becomes a too, too prosperous and egoistic Church. Freedom as soon as it is secured becomes tyranny. A German defeat to-day would have begun with the victory of 1870, for which God was rapturously praised, and with the *Siegestrunkenheit* that started there. Misfortune need not be judgment, nor need defeat; but victory may be. And defeat may be victory.

The irony seems most cruel when it overtakes one who is the slave of no ambition but, like Socrates, is filled with the great idea, or like Christ with the Holy Ghost—men whose passion did not need to be overruled for the Kingdom of Heaven, but was purely and wholly engrossed with it. We are faced with the gigantic and ironic paradox of the Cross, which crushes the best to raise both them and the world.

To the questions stirred by judgment, delicate or palpable, there is no answer in any philosophy even of history. But there is in theology—in a theology that takes its stand, first and last, on the judgment in the Cross. This Act is everywhere in relation with earthly junctures and passions, and everywhere their master, however evasive the mastery be and concealed. Love can easily become impatient of either sublimity or irony, till it find itself in the Cross of Christ. It can become too soft to scorn, and too kind to judge. The devotees of the white passions know little of the red, and nothing of the black. They have not descended into hell. But in Christ's moral, historic, final Cross alone do we learn to interpret the irony of history as the irony of Providence, the tender, portentous smile of a victorious, patient God. If His words are acts, so is that slow smile. Heaven does not laugh loud but it laughs last—when all the world will laugh in its light. It is a smile more immeasurable than ocean's and more deep; it is an irony gentler and more patient than the bending skies, the irony of a long love and the play of its sure mastery; it is the smile of the holy in its silent omnipotence of mercy. The stillness of those heavens that our guns cannot reach is not a circumambient indifference, it is an irony of the Eternal power in sure control of human passion, a sleepless judgment on it, an incessant verdict, very active, mighty, and monitory for those that have ears to hear—yea, very merciful. Greater than the irony in history is the irony over it. Great is the irony of persecution by the Church, of cruelty coming from culture, of corruption from the very success of purity, of a colossal egoism in the wake of much self-denial. But greater and other is the irony of those skies that look down on the whole earth and make its ironies little—look down, so inert yet so ominous, so still yet so eloquent, so vacant yet so charged with the judgment that the Cunctator Maximus is incessantly passing on man—penetrating by its slow insistence, wearing earth down with its monotone of doom. We have that sublime, and ironic, and ceaseless judgment in the irony of Christ before Pilate—all Heaven taking sentence from rude Rome, the chief outcast of the world judging the world with the last judgment of its God.

The non-intervention of God bears very heavy interest, and He is greatly to be feared when He does nothing. He moves in long orbits, out of sight and sound. But He always arrives. Nothing can arrest the judgment of the Cross, nothing shake the judgment-seat of Christ. The world gets a long time to pay, but all the accounts are kept—to the uttermost farthing. Lest if anything were forgotten there might be something unforgiven, unredeemed, and unholy still.

CHAPTER XII

THE CONQUEST OF TIME BY ETERNITY

I BEGAN this book with an outline as overture, I would close it with a *résumé* as coda.

Life begins as a problem, but when it ends well it ends as a faith: a great problem, therefore a great faith. Ordinary experience gives us the first half, it sets a problem; but the second half, the answer of faith to us, comes from God's revelation of grace. As we here pass from the one to the other it should be on large lines, not that we may simply descant on life in a literary way, but that we may magnify the greatness of Christ. Literature after all has but a small Christ; and a small Christ, a small salvation, fits ill to so great a world. And we cannot have a great Christ who is not a theological Christ. The Christ of the world, and of its eternity, must be substantially the Christ of the great creeds. The deeper thought is the more it must theologise. To overcome the world and master life takes all the deep resources of Eternal God—Father, Son, and Holy Spirit. 'When the Gospel is duly preached it is the Trinity that preaches.' Christ, if He is as deep as His religion, is not the great problem, but the great answer.

1. Life, then, is a problem. It offers a task rather than an enjoyment. The soul must be achieved. The kingdom is above all a gift, but it is also a conquest. We are here to fight the good fight rather than to have a good time. The people to whom life is only an excursion, a picnic, a stroll, or a game grow more and more outlanders

in society. And the war will do much to quench that spirit. Most people—more people than ever, at least—feel life's problem to-day more sharply than ever before.

Indeed, some feel nothing else. The trouble with so many serious minds among us is that life is no more than a problem to them. They are loaded with the riddle of it. They are victims of the age of uncertainty and unrest. It is not work that kills, but such worry. What does the life of worry mean but that life is felt to be much more full of problems than of power ?

2. To take another step. The problem is disquieting, anxious, and even tragic. It is not simply interesting and amusing : not like a chess problem, or a mathematical, or a literary, to be solved at arm's length by our wits for the pleasure of the thing. We are in no *Kriegspiel,* but in the real thing always. It touches the nerve. It *is* a problem, it is not a riddle. It has become a war. It involves the realities of life, the things most dear, solemn, searching, commanding. Darkness—is it the cloud of night or the mist of dawn ? Disaster—is it there to burn up life, or to temper and anneal it ; to crush life, or to rouse in us the spirit that overcomes it ? Death —does it explode life or expand it, stifle it or solve it ? Life is not a seductive puzzle ; it is a tragic battle for existence, for power, for eternal life.

There were two powerful thinkers in Germany last century whose influence was not only academic but popular (for they had that gift) ; and they did not only affect Germany but the world. I mean Strauss and Nietzsche. Both were apostles of negation. But the negation of Nietzsche is a far higher and deeper thing than that of Strauss. And it is a more hopeful thing because more thorough. It is a proof of progress that the negation of the one has displaced that of the other, and superseded it. Strauss grows obsolete. He was the supreme rationalist and optimist. He represented civilisation, culture without tragedy, sanity with its aplomb and its self-satisfaction. He came with a Hegelian system into which everything could be fitted, and where everything was right. He saw life as a vast plane in which everything was to be 'placed' or taken up. But Nietzsche saw life as a vast depth, as a throbbing reality, a tragic tangle, a debacle of the soul, and not as a varied landscape or a cosmic process. The engrossing thing in life for him was not in the rational, but in what refused rationality, and could not be placed and appraised. Life was not evolutionary but revolutionary. Its value was more personal; whereas to Strauss it was more processional and mechanical. Nietzsche felt, as millions feel, that life culminated in its tragic experiences, and that whatever solved the tragedy of life solved all life. That is why I say his challenge of Christianity is greater, more incisive, more searching and taxing than that of Strauss, and therefore more promising and more sympathetic, for all his contempt. He was not a spectator but an actor in this tragedy, so much so that it unhinged his mind. To grasp the real, deep tragedy of life is enough to unhinge any mind which does not find God's solution of it in the central tragedy of the Cross and its redemption.

But life's tragic problem to-day is not merely discussed in *salons* by philosophers and their circles, nor by *petits-maîtres* and amateurs of thought; it lays hold of almost every man who takes things seriously at all. And especially it takes religion seriously and gets beyond the Cheeryble brothers. Life is not a riddle for a tea-party, but a battle of blood. It is certainly not a matter of snug optimism in philosophy, nor of mauve religion in fiction.

3. The next step is that there is a solution to the problem. Our battle is not a sport for heaven. I am thinking of the a-theology of Thomas Hardy, and the close of *Tess of the D'Urbervilles*. Life's tragedy is not God's jest. It is working out a real issue with Him. The struggle is not an end in itself. We are not here like

hunters who care everything for the chase and nothing for the quarry. The quest does promise conquest. The riddle of the painful earth has its final answer. The Christian message is that the answer is there, and is the gift of God. It is provided. And it is practical. It is done more than spoken, and done to our hand. We are not asked to waste our labour on the insoluble. At the risk of being called dogmatists the Church, the pulpit, the Gospel are all there to say that there is a solution, that it is given us rather than won by us, and already done and not merely shown. If there is no foregone solution, these voices have no right to speak. But they say there is a solution, and they not only say there is, but they are there to bring it, and give it, and stake life on it. As man dogmatises to nature, God dogmatises to man. 'There remaineth a rest for the people of God.'

4. Still, a step is to be taken which I have partly anticipated. The solution is practical, not philosophical. It is not really an answer to a riddle but a victory in a battle. A life problem cannot be thought out but lived out. Man conquers by faith and not by philosophy. Philosophy itself begins by trusting; it trusts our faculties.

Thought is a mighty and precious power, but on the last things it does more to enlarge our field than to steady our feet. It gives us range, not footing; a horizon rather than a foundation. It does not establish the soul, but widens its vision. It extends our reach more than it fixes our grasp. It therefore often magnifies the problem rather than solves it. Truly, that is a great service. To greaten the problem is to prepare for a great answer. Faith is not there as an asylum for those who are too lazy or shallow to think. But, though thought may tax faith mightily, it cannot do its work. It gives it a grand challenge, but it has not faith's final word. There is something that gives us power to live and conquer, where thought may only raise challenge and doubt. Thought opens a world ahead of us, but faith forces us back into the soul and its case. Faith must be more conservative than thought; for it is deeper. The vaster the world that thought opens, the vaster is the question it puts; and the answers, the solutions, that fitted a small world, go out of date in a large. But the solution, the secret, of the soul, is the same yesterday, to-day, and for ever. It is Christ dead and risen that has the key of life. It is living faith in His living, giving, and saving God.

5. So, the practical solution of life by the soul is outside life. The destiny of experience is beyond itself. The lines of life's moral movement and of thought's *nisus* converge in a point beyond life and history. This world is only complete in another; it is part and prelude of another, and runs up into it, and comes home in it as body does in soul.

What is meant when we speak of another world? We do not mean only one that begins at death. We do not mean a new tract of time beyond the grave, but another order, another dimension, of things, that both haunts the precincts and fills the spaces of this life always.

We may illustrate from that great mirror of life—the stage. History is a grand drama, it is not a mere process. It is not a book of Genesis but a book of Job, not a succession of generations, but one vast act of regeneration. (It is certainly more than a mere school or *palaestra* for training.) It is not a swelling procession of people or of principles. It has a providence, an issue, a teleology, a denouement. And all great drama, Greek or Shakespearean, has a divinity over it for its providence. That was the judgment of these great seers on life. God is in human affairs, and not simply as an immanence (what does that matter?), but as a control. All life has God and His vast providence and purpose in it. Now all dramas are either comedies or tragedies. If life were a great comedy, the grand solution and reconcilement would come in its palpable close. All would be gathered up and finished off there. Life would be rounded, after some jars, with a heavenly smile. We should have but the story with the happy ending, all in one volume. But life is too large, and it moves in curves too great, to be trimmed down and rounded off in our brief first volume. There are two volumes at least. The powers at war in it (if I change the figure) are too vast to settle the eternal issue in a campaign so short.

'History,' says Wellhausen, meaning the course of history, 'takes no account of the good will. Indeed, altogether, it does not reckon with men but with acts. It does not confine the effects of actions to the doer; it punishes folly and weakness heavier than sin. It can make no act as if it had never been. It takes no notice of change of heart. In short, history is, in its effect on the individual, a tragedy; and no tragedy has a satisfying close. And in the case of the prophets, history carried their position far beyond their people—yea, beyond the world.'

If we turn to the modern mind, and if we read the series of Shakespeare's plays in their order, we should see this illustrated as we moved from *As You Like It* to *Hamlet*, *Lear*, and *Othello*. As the passions grow in greatness, the solution at death becomes more incomplete, more of a patchwork. The action is not concluded within the play. It goes sounding on a dim and perilous way beyond. The curtain does not end all. Even if the close be no more than a dim celestial sound of harpers harping on their harps, Shakespeare does stir the prophetic sense of the Divinity throughout all, and the great surmise of a solution beyond. Such serious art issues in religion—the moral realism of tragedy in supernatural faith. And so, as the scale, complexity, and gravity of human life grow in history and civilisation, as the dimensions of the soul expand, the divine solution is pushed outside life more and more. The key is in the Beyond; though not necessarily beyond death, but beyond the world of the obvious, and palpable, and common-sensible. (Yea, beyond the inward it really is.) The solution of all is indicated as outside all. But it is indicated. The unhappy endings do so indicate to the seer's eye. Failure is not yet destruction nor final defeat. Such closes are both prayers and prophecies. They mean that God alone may end things when they become as bad as they are great. 'Real life is always misrepresented by those who wish to make it lead up to a conclusion. God alone may do that. The greatest geniuses have never concluded' (Flaubert).

And so it should always be in great art. Why should any writer throw down before us the sordid, confused, miserable, or tragic in life if he cannot set them in that divine light or its dawn? For writer or reader to be able to linger on these things, and carefully set them out unrelieved and unredeemed, may betoken hard nerves or shrewd sense more than true insight or triumphant faith. We need not demand happy endings if only we are made to feel the atmosphere of moral triumph, the presentiment of a grand consummation, and the dawn of an eternal reconciliation. 'The play, with Shakespeare, is not all. It but shapes for something beyond. And so we take our stand according to the judgment of the Divinity beyond. We believe what we cannot see, and so we are exalted and purged in our outlook on life' (Darrell Figgis on Shakespeare). We settle down at last only in God's estimate of life, God's judgment of it all, God's gift to it, God's product from it. We sit down in His kingdom. The course of history is not the world judgment, as has been too lightly said since Schiller. It is not time that judges time, but eternity always looking in upon time. After death the real judgment! 'But what a terror to add to life!' it may be said. 'Why haunt and cow us thus?' But surely rather, what a hope and joy! Judgment is the grand rectification of all things. Such is the Bible, the

Christian, idea of judgment. It is a joy, a glorious hope. You think of hell and heaven—but think of righteousness, with all things lying glorious in that golden light, and their traffic moving mightily and sweetly in its glow.

Was it not pre-eminently as I have described with the greatest of all life-dramas, the tragedy of Christ? Did the earthly fate of that soul fit its sanctity? Did death make a rounded, closed, finished thing of that life—a thing æsthetically complete like the life of the aged Goethe or Wordsworth? No, indeed. So much so that some have ventured to say He never was, and never claimed to be, Messiah on earth; He was only to be Messiah when He returned from heaven to earth for a new and glorious career. That view is but partly true—true in what it affirms, not in what it denies. It is true in so far as that the only explanation of that death comes from beyond it; not from Christ's earthly teaching among His disciples, but from His posthumous inspiration which made them apostles of a victorious Cross that settled eternal things. That Cross was not for them a martyrdom sealing the past but a redemption securing the future. If the Cross was a mere martyrdom, and ended all, it really upset all. It did not overcome the world. It solved nothing. Nay, it aggravated everything. It deepened the problem. The best of men met the worst of fates and succumbed, and God said nothing and did nothing. No solemn shock of judgment justified Christ or confounded His slayers. His faith was the great illusion. Nay, the Cross alone is no solution without the solution for the Cross itself, the Resurrection, and all its train beyond Christ's death. The solution of life is death shown practically as a victory over death of every kind.

Consider in this light also the vast drama of history. Again remember my object. It is to glorify the creative finality of Christ—not to enlarge on evolution. There are happily still people who ask what all the long and tragic train of history means, what great thing does it intend, what destiny is it moving to, where its close shall be. To what do all things work together ? They ask what is it all worth at last, what is to be the end of earth's long historic day. Is it sheer oblivion or another morning ? Has history a destiny worth all its awful cost ? Do all its large lines converge on anything, its throbbing sorrows, its soaring aspirations, its tragedies sordid or sublime, its dreadful conflicts, its splendid achievements, its miserable failures, its broken hearts and ruined civilisations, its conquests over nature and its collapses into it—do they all curve in some vast trend and draw together to a due close ? Is it an end that can ever make them worth while ? Do they all work together for good and love ? What does man mean ? Or are you so happy with the children, or so engrossed in your enterprises, that you can spare no attention to ask about the movement, the meaning, the fate of the race ? There is a whole type of religion to which such questions are just unintelligible.

When we do rise to ask such questions, where do we find the answer ? Can we find it by questioning our single soul and listening to the voices there ? Because I am saved, or because I am sanguine, because I see an inner light, or hear an inner voice, can I be sure of the salvation of the world ? Or do we find it by studying the whole arena and course of history, so far as gone, and drawing conclusions, making inductions, generalisations, forecasts, from that ? How can we ? Only a small part of history has unrolled. Can we be sure that the long, long future will bear out the hopeful signs we see in the brief past, the narrow present ? Can we observe in the compass of history any convergence of spiritual lines which go out beyond affairs to meet, apparently, in some grand point in the unseen world ? Supposing you did mark such a trend, how do you know that, outside history, some devilish power may not one day strike in and shatter all the lines and drifts that were pointing so hopefully as long as they remained within the sphere of observation? Why should you be sure that the convergence goes on beyond observation for ever? You cannot be sure. What is it in history that makes us believe in man, in a glorious future and a completed destiny for him? Can man explain himself? Can his heart explain him? His poets? Does the mere hero really overcome the whole world, and pluck out for us the heart of the eternal mystery? Can all the heroes put together yield their own secret, yield it so that we need no Saviour, we and they? We may indeed gain some hope from such sources, especially if we are of a hopeful temperament, and live in a hopeful time. But can we reach faith in that way, the eternal victory over the world, the triumphant certainty of a glorious and stable consummation to make us steadfast, immovable, teeming in the work of the Lord?

No, we cannot. If a few choice souls can, the race cannot, a whole Church cannot. For one thing, if history could explain itself, it could explain Christ as a part of it. And, if the general course of history could explain Christ, that would reduce Christ to be but a product of history. Whereas it is more true to say that history is the product of Christ, and Christ explains history as it can never explain Him. That at least is what He believed.

History, man, can only be understood by something which is final in history as well as beyond history, something in it but not of it, given to it but not rising from it, something that stands victorious and creative within it and says, 'You are from below, I am from above. You are evolving from beneath, I am descending from above. I bring God to explain man and complete him, as he can never explain or complete himself. I assure man of his eternal future because it is I who secure it. My great last word is My Deed. My promise is the performance itself. I do not scrutinise time and then infer hope. I bring eternity to redress the balance and change the soul of time. I bring His Word who alone sees man's end, His Deed who alone secures it. I bring the Creator with a new Creation. I am He.'

The world thus finds its consummation not in finding itself but in finding its Master; not in coming to its true self but in meeting its true Lord and Saviour; not in overcoming but in being overcome. We are more than conquerors: we are redeemed.

That is the Word of the Christian Gospel. The great Word of Gospel is not God is love. That is too stationary, too little energetic. It produces a religion unable to cope with crises. But the Word is this—Love is omnipotent for ever because it is holy. That is the voice of Christ—raised from the midst of time, and its chaos, and its convulsions, yet coming from the depths of eternity, where the Son dwells in the bosom of the Father, the Son to whom all power is given in heaven and on earth because He overcame the world in a Cross holier than love itself, more tragic, more solemn, more dynamic than all earth's wars. The key to history is the historic Christ above history and in command of it, and there is no other.

6. This Christ not only assures us of the divine issue of it all: He secures it. The solution is not a promise, not an idea, not an inspiration only; it is a revelation, an achievement, a victory, a creation; it is the supreme act of life, the grand moral act, ever finished, ever being completed, at the centre of all existence.

For the Christ who died had overcome first of all in His own universal soul. It would have been of little use that Christ should advise His disciples to be of good cheer had He not Himself spoken from the peace of the world overcome. It was the constant victory in His soul, rising to the finished victory on the Cross, that gave His precepts their real imperative, and give it to this day. His words draw their worth from His experience, His consciousness, from His soul's work, finished on the Cross but not begun there. We can look back to His words from His work and see that. They are the most precious words in the world because they were spoken by the Man of the Cross, whose every crisis was a vanquished cross, whose Cross was but the crisis of all the crises of His life.

His victory, therefore, did not begin only when He conquered the Cross. He was thus dying and conquering all His life, in word and deed. He never failed to conquer at every crisis of thought or action. These were incessant. He was a man of swift and constant decisions, and He conquered for good and all in the crisis which was the crisis of all the rest. His words do not fail to reflect this inner victory. They are all autobiographical indirectly. So, while living, and before He is crucified, He still says, 'I *have* overcome the world.' Forgiveness, we say, comes by the Cross. But Christ forgave before the Cross. That is because He was always on the redeeming Cross. In the midst of life He was in saving death—in such deaths oft. So the solution from beyond life is really a solution that saturates life. It is above life within it, *au delà de l'intérieur*.

7. All the crises of His life, I have been saying, had themselves a crisis in His death, where the victory and the solution was won once for all. He did not cheer the disciples with the sanguine optimism of the good time coming. It was not a sanguine optimism, but an optimism of actual faith and conquest. It was not the hope of a conquering Messiah soon. 'He is here,' was the Gospel. And so we are not hopeful that the world will be overcome; we know it has been. We are born into an overcome, a redeemed world. To be sure of that changes the whole complexion of life, religion, and action in a way to which to-day we are strange. It is much to be quite sure that the world will one day be righteous; it is more to know that a universal Christ is its perfect

righteousness already. We see not yet all things put under righteousness, but we see Jesus already crowned with that glory and honour. That is Christianity. If it seem absurd, it is only as the peace of God is so in such a world as surrounds us.

8. This word once for all has the note of the infinite and eternal and final, the note of the last reality in all things. The solution in the Gospel is wrought once for all because it was on a world scale, an eternal scale, because He, and He alone of all men, was on such a scale. He was on a scale which made the New Testament writers give Him not only a human and historic influence but a cosmic, nay, an absolute. He was to command not only the race but the universe, and save not only the soul but the whole groaning and travailing creation. That is one reason for believing in miracles, and especially the miracle of the Resurrection. He is King, Subjugator, and Commander both of nature and the soul. And, if He emerge on the soul's experience with the miracle of grace, then in the service of that grace He may emerge also on the soul's world with miracles of power; and especially in His Resurrection. Heaven is not simply the soul lifted abstractly above nature; it is not simply the rule of the spiritual; it is nature compelled to serve the redeemed soul. Christ's miracles are parts, and even functions, of His moral conquest and control of the whole world.

But, however that be, He was, in His victory, the Agent of the race. He did not overcome the world as a cloistered saint might, who conquers it in his solitary soul. He does not bid us go and do likewise. Christ was no mere lone individual and pioneer. He was the soul and conscience of the race. It is by union with Him the race lives. If He overcame the world, it was Humanity that won. If Christ died for all, all died in the act. We rise because He rose; and we rise not like Him but in Him. And what was overcome was not private temptations but the world taken as one godless principle. All the hate in it was now less than the love, since God had come, had conquered, and come to abide in His Spirit. For the conquest was not mere conquest, as by a Stoic hero; it was revelation, redemption, regeneration as by the Lord the Spirit, by the Son of God, in whom men are more than conquerors. We are the beneficiaries of His conquest by union with Him. We are not so much conquerors by His side or in His wake; we are members of Him and His moral victory. Every soul saved is regenerate by the Resurrection (1 Peter i. 3). That is the source of the Spirit of our regeneration—its point of real origin.

9. We may now see why, if life is a problem, its solution is a faith? We cannot solve life by moral thought or effort but by trust, which unites us with the invincible, eternal, moral act of God in Christ. Christianity is not the sacrifice we make, but the sacrifice we trust; not the victory we win, but the victory we inherit. That is the evangelical principle. We do not see the answer; we trust the Answerer, and measure by Him. We do not gain the victory; we are united with the Victor. Faith is not simply contact but communion. We do not simply refer our souls to Christ, we commit them. And to commit our souls to Christ is to confess the Godhead of Christ. It would be idolatry to commit our eternal soul to one who differed from us but in degree. Christ crucified and risen is the final, eternal answer to the riddle of life. One day, when we sit in heavenly places in Christ, we shall see the tangle of life unroll and fall into shape. We shall see death as the key of life. Our own dead could tell us so already. We shall see guilt destroyed; and, with that, death, wrong, darkness, and grief.

The last enemy to be destroyed was guilt. The problem of problems is the moral problem. I wish the mystics and the thinkers could realise that tragedy. The problem is the practical problem of sin. The answer of all is a moral one. It is redemption. The Son of God is He that taketh away by the moral victory of His soul the sin of the world. In Him the world passed its judgment on God, and Christ took it. But still more in Him, God passed His judgment on the world, and Christ took that also. If we have any sense of judgment we have much reason to fear. I cannot understand how any one with any sense of judgment can discard the atonement and live without terror. But, if we have the sense of the holy and the faith of judgment, the faith that Christ took God's judgment on the world, we must be of good cheer. The world is judged for good and all in Christ. The last judgment is by. All our judgments are in its ascending wake.

He has overcome the world. That is the faith which distinguishes the cheery egoist in religion from the humble confessor. That is what gives the Church a lease of life beyond all States and their wars. A world war is less than the world judgment in Christ. And its horror is less dreadful than man's murder of the Son of God. Under everything is that Rock of Ages. Over every tragedy is the eternal reconciliation. The Church's one foundation carries the whole world.

There are many unschooled thinkers who say that an awful catastrophe like this European war is enough to unsettle any belief in a God, a Father, a kingdom of heaven. Nay, but it is the other way. With such Europe, with its negligence of God and His righteousness, with the levity even of the religious mind, the unsettling thing would be if there were no catastrophe. The disquieting thing would be if there were no judgment on materialist civilisations, poor pieties, and shallow politics, and gorgeous getting on, were there no rectification of things by a tremendous surgery, no dreadful excision of the deadly growth that gathers within the nations that forget God. It is all the judgment action of that kingdom of grace for which we pray. By terrible things in righteousness dost Thou answer us, O God of our salvation. When we pray for the kingdom to come, we know not what we ask.

I am not speaking chiefly of the courage that flows from faith. I am thinking of open-eyed faith itself as an act of supreme courage. It is a bold thing to believe in love amidst such a world, with the memory of such a past as we feel in ourselves or trace through history; in the presence of such a holy God as from the Cross makes sin so guilty and judgment so dreadful; with the wretched experience in us and round us of the tough, invincible, recurrent power of evil. It is a bold thing in the face of the proud, progressive, aggressive, warlike, Satanic world. It is an act of supernatural courage, in the face of all that to-day, to believe in the love and grace of God. To some who realise none of these things it may still seem an act of groundless audacity. But, if we do realise them, if we realise God's judgments, we need all the moral courage God can give us to believe in a thing so tremendous as the total victory over such a world already won, and already ours, even if we sometimes relapse. All things are ours, even that victory, that elevation over a world's sin in us; and our very relapses cannot rob us of it. It is easy to believe with a poor sense of what the holy is, of what it makes sin to be, of what the world is, and can do, for the devil. But it needs the supernatural courage of the Cross to believe (at such an hour as this, say,) in the completeness of the Cross and its eternal victory. But there, the more horror, the more hope. The most damning light is the saving light. Therefore, the more holy fear, the more the Cross is working in us; and the sense of the Cross's judgment is the effect of its grace. Faith is more than an individual calm; it is the Church's collective confidence on the scale of the world for the destiny of the world. The evil world will not win at last, because it failed to win at the only time it ever could. It is a vanquished world where men play their devilries. Christ has overcome it. It can make tribulation, but desolation it can never make.

BIBLIOGRAPHY

The Book of Job. And thereon, first, Froude's Essay in *Short Studies:* second, the *Commentaries* of Davidson, Peake, and Strahan.

St. Paul. *Romans VIII.* with *Commentaries.*

Leibnitz. *Essais de Théodicée.* (1710.)

Butler. *Analogy.*

Pope. *Essay on Man.*

Voltaire. *Candide.*

Schopenhauer. *Die Welt als Wille und Vorstellung* (translated by Haldane and Kemp, 1891).

Pfleiderer. *Philosophy of Religion,* chapter **iv.** (Williams and Norgate, 1888.)

Mill. *Essays on Religion.*

Martineau. *Study of Religion.* Book ii. chapter iii. (Clarendon Press.)

Flint. *Anti-Theistic Theories,* viii. (Scribners.)

Bruce. *Apologetics.* Book i. chapters ii. **x.** (Scribners.)

" *Providential Order of the World.* (Scribners.)

Orr. *The Christian View of God and the World.* Lect. v.

Fairbairn. *The Philosophy of the Christian Religion.* Book i. chapters iii. and iv. (Hodder and Stoughton.)

Ward. *Realm of Ends.* (University Press, Cambridge.)

Galloway. *Philosophy of Religion.* Sec. iii. chapters xiv., **xv.**

Siebeck. *Religionsphilosophie.* Theil ii, kapp. iv. and vii.

Kremer. *Das Problem der Théodicée im 18 Jahrhundert.* (Berlin, 1909.)

Otto Lempp. *Das Problem der Théodicée.*

De Maistre. *Les Soirées de St. Pétersbourg,* 1831.